HEALTHY LIVING
FOR TEENS

INSPIRING ADVICE ON DIET, EXERCISE, AND HANDLING STRESS

YOUTH COMMUNICATION
EDITED BY AL DESETTA

Sky Pony Press
New York

Sky Pony Press books may be purchased in bulk at special discounts for sales promotion, corporate gifts, fund-raising, or educational purposes. Special editions can also be created to specifications. For details, contact the Special Sales Department, Sky Pony Press, 307 West 36th Street, 11th Floor, New York, NY 10018 or info@skyhorsepublishing.com.

Sky Pony® is a registered trademark of Skyhorse Publishing, Inc.®, a Delaware corporation.

Visit our website at www.skyponypress.com.

10 9 8 7 6 5 4 3 2 1

Library of Congress Cataloging-in-Publication Data is available on file.

Executive editors: Keith Hefner and Laura Longhine
Contributing editors: Marie Glancy, Nora McCarthy, Maria Luisa Tucker, Tamar Rothenberg, Katia Hetter, Hope Vanderberg, Kendra Hurley, Rachel Blustain, Sasha Chavkin, Andrea Estepa, Virginia Vitzthum, Autumn Spanne, and Holly St. Lifer.
Cover design by Daniel Brount

Print ISBN: 978-1-5107-5990-9
Ebook ISBN: 978-1-5107-5991-6

Printed in the United States of America

Contents

Part Three:
Staying Healthy: Dealing with Stress

Using the Book

INTRODUCTION

In *Healthy Living for Teens*, teens show that it's possible to overcome bad habits and lead healthy lives in a time when substance abuse, junk food, and obesity are major social problems.

In the first part of the book, several writers describe how they fell into unhealthy habits. Edwin Mercado, 17, has been smoking since age 12 and knows he has to quit but can't. Evelyn Gofman hates smoking but finds herself in the dilemma of dating a smoker. To deal with stress and loss in his life, Antwaun Garcia starts abusing alcohol and drugs.

But most of these writers are able to change their bad habits into good ones by making healthier choices. Antwaun realizes that substance abuse, instead of helping him, only brings out his demons, and he finds better ways to deal with his emotions. The anonymous author of "Starving for Acceptance" considers herself "chubby" and wants to look like the skinny girls in her school. She embarks on a dangerous program of losing and then regaining large amounts of weight. Eventually she realizes that being healthy doesn't mean starving yourself or conforming to stereotypical notions of female attractiveness.

In a second story, Antwaun Garcia describes how he was in good shape until age 15. Then, everything changed.

"I would stay out late eating street food, the usual Chinese food, pizza, beef patties, Oreos, and Doritos," Antwaun writes. "I began to gain a whole lot of weight. Between ages 15 and 17, I must have gained about 150 pounds."

Realizing this path is a dead end, he embarks on a rigorous program of working out and sticking to a better diet to get back in shape.

The second part of the book focuses on proper nutrition, the foundation of good health. The teen writers make surprising discoveries about themselves and their diets, while learning how to eat in healthier ways.

When Elsa Ho and her friends take a vacation with no adult supervision, they're thrilled they can make their own food choices.

"We ferociously munched on Doritos and gummy worms," she writes. "Our parents would never allow us to eat junk food right before dinner, but since there were no parents in the house, we did as we pleased." But after a few days, eating whatever they want loses its appeal.

"Not only was the junk food not satisfying, but we . . . felt sluggish, bloated, nauseated, and completely lethargic," Elsa writes. "We yearned for some apples and salad. . . . After my unhealthy vacation, I learned that not caring what I eat will leave me feeling ill."

Seeking to understand her fast food addiction, Chantal Hylton interviews a former commissioner of the US Food and Drug Administration, who explains that most packaged and restaurant food contains sugar, fat, and salt to get us hooked.

The anonymous author of "My Hood Is Bad for My Health" wonders why healthy food is scarce in poor neighborhoods and describes the difficulties of living with a grandmother who cooks mainly with meat and oil.

Horrified by how animals are treated after watching a video on slaughterhouse practices, Suzy Berkowitz tries to become a vegetarian. But having grown up among carnivores, becoming a complete vegetarian isn't a viable option, so she makes her contribution by boycotting meat at fast-food restaurants.

The third section of the book looks at how teens can stay healthy by dealing with stress instead of allowing it to rule their lives and develop into bad habits.

Viveca Shearin overcomes her fear of having an asthma attack, realizing she can't live her life in a bubble. Cynthia Orbes deals with problems by playing vigorous games of handball. Niya Wilson turns to yoga to deal with stress while Ashunte Hunt writes poetry. In the book's final story, Emily Orchier spends so much time lying on the couch in a deep depression that she worries her mother will soon have to dust her. But then she starts taking long walks, her mood lifts, and she realizes how exercise and emotional health are inextricably linked.

Healthy Living for Teens will help teens understand the basics of good health and learn practical ways to achieve it.

PART ONE

GETTING HEALTHY:
GIVING UP BAD HABITS

TALES OF A 17-YEAR-OLD SMOKER

By Edwin Mercado

I smoked my first cigarette when I was 12. My father, who smokes, was cleaning up the day after a party. He lit a cigarette, took two drags, and just left it in the ashtray. When he left the room to go to sleep, I saw my opportunity. It was a spur-of-the-moment thought. "Edwin, take a drag," I said to myself.

I guess I wanted to try it because just about everyone in my family smokes or used to smoke: my father, mother, grandfather, aunts, uncles, and my older sister. Then I thought, "But what if you get caught?" I was going crazy wondering whether I should take a drag.

I finally decided to go for it, so I took about five drags of the cigarette. My first impression of smoking was terrible. The taste was nasty and I felt like throwing up. But there was something about it I liked. Smoking made me get a light-headed rush and that felt kind of good. I wanted to feel that same rush again. So I started stealing cigarettes from my father and smoking them in my room or the bathroom.

I was soon smoking about four cigarettes a day, but it wasn't until I turned 14 that I started buying cigarettes. Since I started getting a whole bunch of facial hair, I looked old enough to buy them.

The taste was nasty and I felt like throwing up.

I didn't have much money, so I had to buy loosies, which at the time cost 25 cents for one cigarette. It became a habit, buying about three cigarettes in the morning and three after school. Since I was 14—I'm 17 now—I've hardly gone a day without smoking a cigarette, except when I'm sick. I'm addicted.

It's been hard to hide my smoking from my parents, because I want to smoke when I'm home. The first time I got caught, it was because I had left cigarettes in my pocket. I had bought one and taken one each from my mother and grandfather.

My mom had come into my room one morning to wake me up for school. She saw my jeans. "You want me to wash these?" she asked. Without thinking I said yes, so she emptied out my pockets and that's when she found the cigarettes.

I was brushing my teeth when she barged into the bathroom and said in a loud, scary mother voice, "What the heck is this?"

I dropped the toothbrush.

"Ahh," I said. "They're not mine, I found them."

"Yeah, right," she said and smacked me hard upside my head.

When my mother gets angry, it's not a pretty sight. Her face gets red and her lips turn smaller and it scares the hell out of me. That whole day I was in shock because she caught me and I didn't know what to do. It was the worst feeling in the world when my mother found out I was smoking. I felt like the world was going to end.

When I got caught, I thought about stopping. I did stop for about a week, because all I could think about was getting caught again. But I got a little less worried, and I started up again.

I wish I had my mom's willpower. When my mother used to smoke, she smoked about four cigarettes a day. She didn't really like it, but it became a habit. One day she said, "That's it for me. I'm going to stop smoking." And she did. Within a week, she had stopped totally. My father, though, has been smoking for over twenty years. He always says he's going to stop, but he doesn't.

My parents have caught me about five times with a cigarette in my mouth and about thirty times by finding cigarette butts in my room or in the laundry room. I get screamed at and punished. As punishment for smoking, my parents don't give me money for a while. Plus, I've gotten about a hundred lectures, where they ask, "Where do you get your cigarettes from?" or say, "I'm going to kick your rear if you keep on smoking."

I've heard it all, so now I lie to save myself the lectures. When I leave butts around or have a cigarette smell when I come out of the bathroom, I just deny it.

I've tried to smoke outside my house, but when I come back, my parents ask me, "Where were you?" I say, "I needed some fresh air." They know I'm lying. I can see it in their eyes; they look at me as if I'm stupid. I feel real bad when I have a hard time with my parents, and I tell myself I'm not going to smoke anymore, but I still do.

I think my parents don't want me to smoke because they know how hard it can be to stop. And they don't want me to try smoking other things like weed.

I know smoking is bad for me because I'm only 17 and I can't even play three games of basketball. I usually have to stop because I can't breathe. I don't want to be in the hospital in ten years, coughing up phlegm because I'm a smoker.

Smoking already makes me sick. From time to time, I get a sore throat that feels like I swallowed glass. When I get this sore throat, I tell myself I'm going to stop smoking but all I do is cut down. And when my sore throat is gone, I start smoking as much as before. As I write this, I'm getting a sore throat. It makes me want to stop, but I keep smoking anyway.

Smoking is also bad for my wallet. The first day I found out that they raised the prices for cigarettes, I felt like crying since I now go through a pack in about two days, three at the most.

> I get a sore throat that feels like I swallowed glass.

Packs of cigarettes used to cost $3.25 or $3.50, and now they cost $7 or even more. (I also buy three packs of Doublemint every day so my breath won't stink.)

I know I'm wasting my money on something like that, because I know smoking isn't good for me, but I can't stop. I don't think I could go a day without having a cigarette. What I like about smoking is that it calms me down. If I'm pissed off about something, I just smoke a cigarette and I'm not so mad.

When I don't have a cigarette, I get very cranky. And I don't know why, but my stomach starts to crave food. I could have just finished eating, but I get hungry. It's not a good feeling.

A few of my friends smoke, but they're not addicted like me. They only smoke sometimes. They tell me "Yo, Ed, you need to stop smoking. You gonna just die one of these days." I tell them, "Yeah, I need to stop, but I can't."

I know there are patches and gum that supposedly help you stop smoking. I haven't tried those patches or gum myself, but I know people who say they're a waste of time and money. I think if you really want to stop smoking, you have to do it on your own.

I plan to stop smoking soon, maybe by January. I'll make that my New Year's resolution. I plan to stop little by little, maybe cutting down at first to about three cigarettes a day. But if that doesn't work, I'll go cold turkey. I know if I go cold turkey, I'm going to go through some hard times because I'm going to have the urge to smoke, but I'm going to do whatever it takes to stop.

Edwin was 17 when he wrote this story.

Stop the Smoke!

By Evelyn Gofman

I've lived around cigarette smoke all my life, but that doesn't mean I've gotten used to it. I've disliked the smell of cigarette smoke ever since I can remember.

My dad smokes. Fortunately, he doesn't smoke in front of me or in the house. He goes outside—no matter what the weather is like.

My mom and I wish he'd quit. We've talked to him about it, and so have his doctors; they told him that stopping smoking would help his back problems. We even sent him to hypnosis sessions. But after twenty years, the habit's too strong to kick.

I worry about my dad. Seeing his struggle with cigarettes made me want to learn about the harm they can do and how addictive they are. The more I found out, the more I hated the idea of ever putting that stick-shaped object in my mouth.

Cigarettes contain nicotine, an addictive chemical that affects the body and the mind and keeps people hooked. And tobacco companies' own reports admit that they add ammonia, which makes the brain absorb more nicotine than it normally would.

Some companies actually add licorice and cocoa to ciga-rettes, not for taste reasons, but because they help you inhale the smoke and get the nicotine further into your body.

8

Because nicotine is so addictive, even people who want to quit often can't. It takes about two or three days for most of the nicotine to leave a smoker's body after he or she stops smoking, but intense cravings usually follow as symptoms of withdrawal.

But cigarettes are more than just an annoying habit that's hard to break. According to the Centers for Disease Control, the health problems caused by cigarettes are responsible for more deaths in the United States than AIDS, suicide, fires, alcohol, and all illegal drugs combined.

One of the worst smoke-related diseases is emphysema, the narrowing of passages in the lungs, because there's no known cure for it and it only gets worse over time.

> Cigarettes cause more U.S. deaths than AIDS, suicide, fires, alcohol, and drugs.

Then there are the lung cancer cases, about 87 percent of which are smoke-related. People who smoke are also a lot more likely to develop cancer in other parts of their body, such as their throat, bladder, and mouth.

Knowing the dangers of smoking made me hate it even more. And because I had such a strong dislike of cigarettes, I was never attracted to boys who smoke. When I saw a group of guys with smoke in their faces, I just assumed I wouldn't find common ground with them.

Last winter, though, I met this guy, Roman, who I came to really like. I couldn't resist his wittiness and sense of humor. I enjoyed spending time with him, going to the movies or Central Park.

When I first met him, he had a cigarette in his mouth, but once we started hanging out, he didn't smoke in front of me. Sometimes he'd wait up to five to six hours for a smoke. Only now do I understand what he went through for me.

Five months after we met, we started going out, and the reality set in on me: I was dating a smoker.

Me? Evelyn? I was going against all my standards and values. Smoking was a big "no-no!" Yet here it was, in my face. I was dating someone who did the very thing my dad did, the thing I hated.

Since we were spending more time together, sometimes Roman would smoke around me. It still drives me crazy when he smokes. I feel like my own lungs are corroding when I see a cigarette between his lips—where my lips should be.

I told him he should quit. I told him I hated it. I told him that he was killing himself! When I asked him whether he thinks about tobacco's harms when he's smoking, Roman said, "No. It's much easier that way."

Reality set in on me: I was dating a smoker.

I thought I'd persuade him that smoking can do lots of damage, but he still insists cigarettes can't do anything but addict him.

I thought maybe he'd take me more seriously if I tried it for myself. Even though I despise the smell of cigarettes and know how harmful the habit can be, I wanted to experience it firsthand.

I wanted to understand what the attraction was. I knew that people said smoking made them feel calmer and more relaxed. I was curious. And I figured once I knew all the sides to smoking, I could be more comfortable criticizing the living hell out of it.

So last spring, hanging out with Roman in New York City, I tried my first cigarette. I took the cigarette between my index and middle finger, barely able to hold it in place, and put it to my lip-glossed lips. I felt like a 5-year-old who just discovered something new to play with. "This is too ridiculous," I thought.

It took a few seconds before I finally inhaled and felt . . nothing! I thought maybe a party of senses would go off in my mouth, but that didn't happen. I tried it again to make sure I did it right. There was a bad taste and a gasp-like feeling in my throat. I coughed.

"That wasn't so bad," I said to Roman, who was half-amused.

But I didn't see what was so special about it either. I never finished that cigarette.

A few weeks later, I tried it again. Don't get me wrong, I wasn't trying to get hooked—I was only trying to see what was so "great" about smoking. But trying it this time, I was only reminded that it tasted awful. Again, I didn't feel anything exciting. "Is that all?" I said. My curiosity ceased.

But according to the American Lung Association, every day, three thousand teens in this country smoke their first cigarette. Many go on to pick up the habit; at least four million teens currently smoke. I'm not joining them. But I think trying it for myself made me realize how easily people can pick up the habit without realizing what they're doing.

Roman tried his first cigarette when he was just 5. He credits it to the older kids in his neighborhood in St. Petersburg, Russia, who were already smoking. "Most of the younger kids started smoking to copy them," he said. He started smoking regularly at 15 and now, at 19, smokes 10 cigarettes a day.

Roman started smoking because people around him were, and that's how my dad started, too. By the time he was in college, every one of his friends smoked. After a while, he joined in—and got hooked.

For young people, friends are our support system, our advice givers, and our party people. Whether it's obvious peer pressure or not, it's easier to relate to your friends when you all do the same things. Smoking also seems "cool" to a lot of people who'd rather smoke than stick out of the crowd.

Once people pick up the habit of smoking, it gets increasingly hard to quit. And the younger people are when they start smoking, the more likely they are to develop severe nicotine addiction.

Roman says quitting is really difficult. "Not smoking for a day, my head feels like it's going to pop," he told me. "In a week without tobacco, I'll jump on people."

After seeing addiction in action—watching my father banished to the porch when it's below zero, so he can smoke, and seeing Roman barely able to stand five smoke-free hours with me—I'm convinced smoking is evil. Now, if only I can convince them.

Evelyn was 15 when she wrote this story. She later published her own zine, graduated from college, and went on to pharmacy school.

HOW I QUIT FAST FOOD. . . AND LIVED TO WRITE ABOUT IT

By Carmen Rios

Until I read *Chew on This: Everything You Don't Want to Know About Fast Food*, a book for young people by Eric Schlosser and Charles Wilson about what we eat, I was one of the many teens eating fast food almost every day. I loved fast food. Eating it was like getting a special gift.

By the time I was in middle school, I'd gotten so tired of eating the Latin food my mom made every day: arroz blanco con abichuelas (white rice with beans) and pollo frito (fried chicken). I preferred McDonald's. I knew that eating too much fast food could make me fat, but I didn't see myself getting any bigger (I only weigh 105 pounds). Plus, the food was delicious.

I wanted to eat McDonald's every day but I couldn't afford it. So I waited until every Wednesday, when my stepfather got paid, and every Friday, when my mother got paid. I'd go to school excited on those days because, at the sound of the bell, I'd be going home to get at least $6 to spend at McDonald's.

My sister and I would rush out of the house and speed walk down our block, turn right, and walk three blocks to

13

our neighborhood McDonald's. On our way there, we'd anxiously talk about what we wanted to eat. The Big Mac meal was our favorite, and we almost never got tired of it.

But when I craved chicken, I'd order the five-piece Chicken Selects meal and my sister would order a "Number 2," the meal with two cheeseburgers, fries, and a beverage (we always chose Coke). All we had to do next was choose the size of the meal (usually medium). After we ate, sometimes we'd get back in line and order apple pies and a medium vanilla shake.

After I got a job last January, I promised myself that I wouldn't waste my money on fast food because I didn't want to get fat. I also wanted to spend my money on clothes and things to decorate my room. But the food was so hard to resist. Right after I got my paycheck every other Friday, I'd stop at a McDonald's or KFC. The next day, I'd bring my sister and my friend along with me and buy them lunch.

Sometimes I'd spend half my paycheck on fast food. I'd spend $6 one day and another $6 the next. Then I'd get hungry in the middle of the night and my sister and I would head out to McDonald's for a late-night meal (it's open until 1 a.m.).

Once I spent my whole paycheck ($135) on fast food. It started off with me buying just one meal. The next day, I asked myself, "What's another $6?" And in the end, I thought to myself, "I wasted everything else on food. What's the point of saving $20? Might as well waste that on food, too!"

> I spent my whole paycheck ($135) on fast food.

Sometimes I'd eat at McDonald's every single day, and not even the movie *Super Size Me*, about a man who only ate McDonald's food every day, scared me into stopping. The movie started off with a perfectly healthy person and ended with the same person—except that he was fat and had heart problems, all because he ate every meal at McDonald's.

In fact, the movie made me crave McDonald's. I watched the guy ordering a meal and I could almost smell the French fries and taste the Big Mac sauce. I wanted so badly to eat his food.

When I saw him throwing up, I told myself the movie was unreal. Who actually eats McDonald's three times a day every day and "super sizes" the meal whenever they're asked if they want the largest meal size? I usually ate fast food two or three times per week, and I never super sized anything. "It's no wonder he got sick!" I told myself.

But then I read *Chew on This* last April. The book disgusted me to the point of wanting to throw up. I was shocked to learn about how the animals we eat in these fast-food restaurants are killed.

First, the chickens are fed a grayish mixture of old pretzels and cookies covered with a layer of fat to make them gain more weight, according to the book. This causes many chickens to die of a heart attack. The rest are tied upside down by their legs to a chain and thrown into a tank of water that's charged with electricity.

That's supposed to make them unconscious, but the chickens that aren't properly shocked have to live through the rest. They're carried to a blade that slits their throats. Then they're dunked into a tank of boiling water.

Cows that are turned into hamburger meat are also badly mistreated. They're placed in feedlots. One feedlot can hold up to 100,000 cattle, which means the cows are crowded very close together. They don't eat fresh, green grass. Instead, they are fed special grain designed to fatten them quickly. I cried when I read about this cruelty. I couldn't believe I was a part of it.

The book also made me worry about obesity, which I've learned is a condition characterized by excessive body fat. It's a growing problem in this country. Did you know that there are 2.8 million deaths every year related to obesity? (People who are obese can develop diabetes and other health problems.)

I believe the obesity problem is connected to the number of McDonald's around the world—38,700 restaurants in 120 countries—and their cheap prices.

A McDonald's Big Mac meal didn't sound tempting or delicious anymore. Every time I thought of eating in a fast-food restaurant, I couldn't help but think of the cows and chickens. It made me feel guilty and nauseous. Right after finishing the book in April, I changed the way I eat. I haven't been back to McDonald's, not even once.

> A Big Mac meal didn't sound tempting anymore.

Instead, I've been going to Subway and ordering the 6-inch meatball sandwich on Italian bread, with American cheese, lettuce, and tomato. I thought that Subway would be a fresh and healthy alternative to Big Macs and fries. But in an interview with *Chew on This* co-author Chuck Wilson, I learned that my Subway meatballs probably came from the same factories as McDonald's hamburger meat.

Now, I'm confused about what I can eat. There are no restaurants in my neighborhood where I can eat healthy food. Even if there were, I've learned from experience that eating healthy usually means eating something that I think tastes disgusting.

Still, when I get hungry during the night, I make myself a salad or I eat fruit that my mom or I bought. I still get to eat what I want, but I make sure I'm not overdoing it. I feel much better about myself and I feel healthier—fresh, clean, and not as heavy. And with the extra money I have, I can buy more clothes, shoes, and beauty supplies.

haven't given up all junk food—yet. I think it'll be difficult for me to give up soda and candy because I like to drink Pepsi and eat Snickers bars. But I bet I'll end up cutting down on junk food slowly, thanks to this book. And I'll make sure that any child I have doesn't fall into the hands of McDonald's.

I don't think McDonald's should take all the blame for the increase in obesity and health problems across the country, though. Adults can choose if they want to eat McDonald's or not. Nobody is forcing them. They can say no at any moment, just like I did. Most people know what eating fast food can do to them, but they still continue to eat it.

But I don't think McDonald's should advertise to kids any more. If kids eat McDonald's when they are toddlers, they are likely to eat it for the rest of their lives, according to the book. If this happens, animals will keep getting treated badly and the earth will be populated with obese people.

Chew on This definitely made me think about what I eat. "The title of the book, *Chew on This*, says it all," said coauthor Charles Wilson. "We just want kids to think about something they take for granted in everyday life."

So that's what I'm trying to do. Eric Schlosser, the book's other author, told me I don't have to stop eating fast food but I should treat it like a special treat. "You don't want to die," he told me in a recent interview. "You want to do everything you can to live a good, long, healthy life. That means knowing what you eat."

Carmen was 18 when she wrote this story.

WHAT'S WRONG WITH FAST FOOD?
By Carmen Rios

After I read *Chew on This,* the book that convinced me to stop eating at McDonald's, I was excited to interview Eric Schlosser, one of the book's authors.

NYC: Why do you write about fast food?
Eric Schlosser: I became curious because I ate fast food a lot, but I didn't know where it came from. Once I learned about the food, I wrote Fast Food Nation (his best-selling book on the fast-food industry). I decided to write Chew on This for kids because I felt the information needed to get out to the kids who the fast-food companies are marketing to.

NYC: What's the problem with teens eating fast food?
Schlosser: The fast-food companies target children and teenagers. These companies know that children and teenagers are developing eating habits they're going to have for the rest of their lives. So the companies want to get people while they're young so that they buy these foods for the rest of their lives.

I have no problem with an adult getting a triple cheeseburger and a large order of fries if that's what they want to do. But I think that these companies shouldn't be marketing to children and young teens because eating this food can affect the rest of their lives.

Have you ever seen a fast-food ad that shows where the food comes from? You'll never see a fast-food ad with an obese person going to hospital for gastric bypass surgery. What they show is happy families and happy teenagers, and they're all really thin.

NYC: What do you want kids to do?
Schlosser: I'm not trying to tell kids what to eat. I'm just trying to tell them what they are eating and what it could do to them. Hopefully kids will change some of their habits and live in a way that ensures they'll be healthy and have a long life.

> If you're obese by age 13, odds are you'll be obese for life.

NYC: What happens if you eat too much fast food?
Schlosser: If you eat a lot of high-fat, highly processed, high-calorie food, and you eat it all the time and you don't exercise, you're going to become overweight, and perhaps obese. If you're obese by age 13, odds are you're going to be obese for the rest of your life. And the health problems that come with being obese are just terrible: increased risk of heart disease, increased risk of cancer, of diabetes, of asthma.

NYC: How bad is the obesity problem?
Schlosser: In the last forty years, the obesity rate among American toddlers has doubled. Among American children ages 6 to 11, it's tripled. The CDC (Centers for Disease Control) thinks that one of every three American children born in 2000 will develop diabetes because they're overweight, and one of every two Latino and African American children will develop diabetes.*

---

* This interview was conducted in 2006/7. As of 2019, the CDC was reporting that 1 in every 5 American (adults and children) are affected by obesity. For children and adolescents ages 2 through 19, the prevalence of obesity is nearly 18.5%, or 13.7 million. Prevalence in 2 to 5-year-olds is 13.9%, 6 to 11-year-olds is 18.4%, and 12 to 19-year-olds is 20.6%.

The worst impact of this food is being felt in minority communities and poor communities. The fast-food chains are very aggressively targeting the children of the poor, particularly Latino and African American children.

NYC: Is there hope?
Schlosser: Absolutely. Ultimately, it's going to be so expensive if we don't change what children are being fed and if we don't end this obesity epidemic. The cost of having to take care of so many people with diabetes, of so many people with heart problems, is going to be enormous.

NYC: Your favorite meal is French fries, a cheeseburger and a chocolate shake. Why do you still eat fast food?
Schlosser: I love French fries. If I were only allowed one last meal, it would be a cheeseburger, French fries—crispy—and a chocolate shake. But just because you love something doesn't mean you should eat it every day. Ideally, you would come up with a diet where something like a hamburger or French fries would be a special treat you'd have every now and then.

> If the food is bad, it becomes part of you.

NYC: How often do you eat fast food?
Schlosser: I have French fries once or twice a month (at In-N-Out Burger, a California fast food restaurant where the food is made fresh). If you totally deny yourself the things you absolutely love, you're going to crave them even more. When you finally break, you might have them every day for a month. I get a fix of French fries, just enough so I don't need to have them every day.

NYC: Other than not eating McDonald's, how can we fight against fast food?
Schlosser: The most important thing is to know what you're eating, where it comes from and what it can do to your body.

Food is probably the single most important thing you buy during the course of a day. It's more important than any clothes or music you're going to buy. If those things are bad, you can get rid of them. But if the food is bad, it becomes part of you.

Carmen was 18 when she interviewed Eric Schlosser.

CLEAN AND KIND OF SOBER

By Antwaun Garcia

When I was a kid, I noticed how family members picked up
a cigarette whenever they felt stress or got mad. My mom
would hand me her boggy (cigarette) and tell me to flush it
down the toilet. One day, when I was 9, I closed the bathroom
door and smoked it.

I figured that if my parents saw me smoking, they'd laugh,
like parents do when they watch a little girl walk in high heels
impersonating her mother. But soon I used cigarettes the same
way my parents did—to feel better.

When I was 10, my life got stressful. My friend Ricky died
in a fire, and I went into foster care, moving to my aunt's
house in Queens, because my mom was using drugs.

When I couldn't read a book my aunt gave me, thought
about how my dad used to hit my mom, or wondered what
my mom was doing on the streets, I couldn't wait to smoke a
cigarette. Sometimes I even sneaked a little alcohol. At family
parties my grandma had let us try it, and it made me feel loose.

Then, when I was 13, my best friend, Jarrel, killed himself.
After he died, I drank a bunch of Bacardi and sat out on my
terrace crying, confused and lost, thinking about my friends'

deaths, not being with my parents or brothers, and feeling isolated instead of loved.

I felt completely alone. I doubted anyone could understand me or all that I had gone through.

After Jarrel died, I wrote many poems about guilt, death, and anger. I found that writing helped me vent emotions.

But the next year, when I got to high school, my boys put me on to something even better: smoking weed. I loved it from the first. We cut class, went to my boy's crib, and smoked about four blunts. I took a mean pull, and after the second pull, I didn't want to pass it around.

In my first two years of high school, I cut class over 300 times and had a 55 average. I liked smoking so much because I never thought about my past or my life when I was high. I just thought about food and what I was going to do when I got home.

I smoked mostly by myself, because when I was smoking with my friends, I would come out with thoughts that I later regretted sharing. I didn't want my boys to know me too well. By 15, I was lighting up by myself in a park far from my neighborhood.

By 17, I was also drinking a lot, taking Bacardi or Hennessy to school in water bottles or drinking after school in a park. I felt lonely, frustrated, angry, and helpless.

I thought it best to drink alone so I didn't show anyone my sadness or get in trouble. When I drank I wanted to fight. If I had liquor in me, I didn't care who the dude was, I threw the hands. With every fight, the anger of my childhood ran through my body. I didn't like who I was, but fighting, drinking, smoking, and writing were the only ways I knew of to deal with my emotions.

Then, when I was 18, I met a girl in my high school. She was a Dominican mami, a natural beauty, intelligent, loved to laugh, and had a beautiful smile. We had two classes together and eventually started dating.

Together we went shopping, to movies and amusement parks, and on picnics in Flushing Meadows. At night we would sit in a park and talk for hours, or bug out in hotels, ordering Pizza Hut and watching movies and having pillow fights. We couldn't get enough of one another.

But my habits started to affect our relationship. Every time I drank, the anger I bottled in came out. On the phone, she would hear me breathing hard and ask, "Antwaun, are you okay?" I'd tell her about a fight I had, usually because I was smoking or drinking.

She realized that smoking and drinking brought out the demon in me, which we were both scared of. My girl would cry because she felt helpless to calm or console me, and I'd get mad at myself for putting her through pain.

Finally one day she told me, "Antwaun, you know I love you, right?"

"Yes!" I replied.

"I love you so much that it hurts. So you have to choose—your habits or me."

I didn't know what to say but I was thinking, "Antwaun, you're losing someone important, and for what? Choose her before you lose her!" So I told her I would stop.

I never completely stopped drinking. (My girl sometimes drank, too, and we'd have a few drinks together.) But I made a major effort to keep my cups under control. Smoking I stopped completely, because I didn't need to escape my reality when I was with her.

As I let her get to know me, she helped me let out some of the feelings I kept inside. To help her understand why I was so angry, I told her about my past.

We talked for hours about each other's pasts, even though her past wasn't like mine. She listened to me, so I felt at ease coming out with everything. I learned how to talk about my feelings rather than hide from them.

Whenever I started to cry, she would tell me, "You don't have to tell me if you're not ready," because she knew I hated crying. I would hold my head back and cover my eyes, and she would hug me and say, "It's okay to cry. I'm here. Everything is fine."

Whatever I didn't tell her about myself, she read in my articles. She kept a book of all my articles and saved them next to her journal and baby pictures. I also kept writing down all my emotions to prevent that feeling of pressure from holding too much in.

> Every time I drank, the anger I bottled in came out.

With my girl's help, I became more focused in school and my life started to look clearer. I was good.

After two years, my girl became depressed due to family issues. Then she moved away. We broke up. After that, I fell into a deep depression that lasted for months. I felt alone and lost. I had no clue of what I wanted to do in life.

I started drinking and smoking again, fell off in school, and didn't wash because I wanted to look like I felt: dirty and pathetic. I was always mad. I stopped writing and let my pain eat at me. My cravings for fast food became real serious, too. Whenever I went to Micky D's, I ordered up to $8 worth of food from the dollar menu. If I ordered Chinese food, I got an egg roll to go with every dish. I gained almost 20 pounds that February. Now I was depressed, confused, alone, failing school—and fat!

Gradually, I got disgusted by myself and tired of always being depressed. I was walking around in small T-shirts with a gut that hung low. My clothes felt tight. I felt like Homer Simpson with waves and a $5 tee.

I started wondering, "How am I going to get over my depression? What direction am I heading in life?" I wasn't the man I wanted to be. Getting high all the time was not helping me to be at peace. Finally, I couldn't stand myself anymore. I knew I had to change.

It helped when my ex and my mom called and reminded me of my good points. "You always had a presence when you entered a room," my ex told me. My mom said she thought of me as a determined guy who never let anyone stand in his way. I began to remember my good characteristics. I am a funny, determined, caring, real dude with a passion to write and a gift for making people smile.

> Getting high all the time was not helping me to be at peace.

I decided to test myself to see if I could stop smoking weed. I started slowly, going a day without smoking by keeping myself busy. I avoided the weed spots, went to school, the library, and home.

I would get the urge to smoke at night. My anger had always given me energy. Without it, I felt lifeless and exhausted sometimes, as if the life force had drained out of me. I almost felt like if I didn't smoke or drink, I wouldn't wake up and feel alive.

But when I got the urge to drink, cry, or smoke, I took long, 45-minute showers. It's a good thing my aunt didn't have to pay the water bill! I also started taking care of myself, putting on my jewelry, which I'd left on the dresser when I was depressed, and slowing down my eating to three meals a day.

I started a workout regimen—running up and down steps, doing push-ups and sit-ups. I started to feel good physically. Seeing that I could take control of my life made my confidence grow. As I felt better, I started to keep busier and be more social. Each change made other changes happen. A year later, I'm still in the process of getting myself back.

Now I keep myself on the move—running in the morning, going to work in the afternoon. On weekends I chill with friends who don't smoke or drink, play basketball with my sister and take my little cousins to the movies. I don't have time to be alone and drink and smoke and reminisce about painful things.

The last time I smoked weed was four months ago. I was at my brother's apartment in Harlem. We ordered Chinese food, and one of my boys brought over an NBA game. We passed around some weed and drank orange juice and vodka while playing video games and conversing about sports and music. I didn't turn down the weed, because it didn't seem like a big deal to smoke one time with friends.

But the next morning I felt physically sick. I was coughing hard and spitting nonstop. That turned me off to smoking. Since then I haven't smoked weed at all.

When I saw my brother again in November and he was smoking weed, I passed it up. When I turned it down, I felt powerful. I knew I could overcome my addiction to smoking weed. I was strict with myself and I stopped.

Since then, I've also cut down smoking cigarettes (to one or two a month) and I don't drink recklessly to deal with stress—just when I'm at a party or celebration.

Both my parents have bad lungs and livers and are perfect examples of what I don't want for myself. My father is sick and paralyzed on the left side of his face, but he still smokes and drinks. Now I realize that my parents may have gotten addicted to smoking, using crack, and drinking the same way I started: to cope with feelings of loneliness, anger, and fear.

I can't say I won't have any more depressions, or that the urge to drink or smoke won't ever overtake me, because I don't know what life has in store, but I know I've made a big change. I feel more in control of myself than ever before.

Antwaun wrote this story when he was 19.
He later attended college and worked in retail.

WHAT DRUGS DO TO YOU (EVEN THE LEGAL ONES)

YC Staff

To understand more about how drugs affect teenagers, we interviewed Dr. James A. Hall, a professor of pediatrics and behavioral health at the University of Iowa in Iowa City. Hall has spent many years researching teenage drug use.

Q: How do I know if I have a problem with drugs or alcohol?
A: There are several warning signs that drug dependence is destroying your ability to live a healthy, happy life.

If you drink or use drugs when you're alone, can't trust yourself to get through certain situations without having to use, or can't remember things that happened when you were high, you should seek help.

If your drug use and hangovers cause problems for you at work or in school (being late, getting loaded instead of studying, falling behind, or getting kicked out), you are also on dangerous ground.

Another sign you are in trouble is when drugs begin destroying your relationships: Your friends or parents or foster parents are on your back about your temper, mood swings, unreliability, or inability to pay attention and stay alert. Or you lie to people about what you've been doing and prefer getting high to being with people who care about you.

You need help if you have to get high in order to feel good or have fun, or if you turn to pills, pot, or alcohol after fights or confrontations to calm down or feel better. Building up a tolerance is also sign of physical addiction: When you need more and more of something in order to get the same effect, you are getting addicted.

> Another sign of trouble is when drugs destroy your relationships.

Q: Are foster youth at greater risk for abusing substances than other teens?
A: Yes. Family troubles increase the risk that a teen will turn to drugs or alcohol to manage his or her feelings of loss, rejection, and pain. Also, many youths in care have parents or caretakers who used drugs. Having a role model who abuses drugs or alcohol increases the risk that you will copy that behavior.

Q: What's so bad about smoking weed or popping pills like cold medicines?
A: Adolescence is a time when you figure out who you are as an individual in society. You go from having external controls (other people telling you what to do) to internal controls (making decisions and thinking things through for yourself). Kids who are on drugs—even marijuana—can't handle these challenges very well because they aren't able to figure out their problems and interpret the world with a clear head.

If you spend a lot of time smoking, you will have delays in learning how to cope with life and how to solve problems, and be slower in developing the confidence and skills you need to overcome the obstacles every adult encounters. When you come down, all the same problems are still there.

Also, many studies show marijuana use interferes with learning. You're slower to understand and respond to things when you're high and get really bad at remembering things. This makes it more difficult to do well in school, to keep yourself safe, and to analyze situations so you can make good decisions.

> You need help if you get high to feel good or have fun.

Even over-the-counter medications can be harmful if you're taking more than you're supposed to take, or taking them for a reason other than the problem that the medicines are designed to help. (Like, if you're taking cold medicine when you don't have a cold!) Many over-the-counter drugs can be every bit as dangerous as street drugs if you take too much.

Q: What's the difference between taking street drugs and the medications doctors prescribe?
A: Lots of teenagers do street drugs or use over-the-counter drugs because they have an underlying condition such as depression, attention deficit hyperactivity disorder, or a learning disorder. They medicate themselves to get more energy, to focus or concentrate, or to feel calmer or happier.

The problem is that illegal drugs have many unpredictable side effects that can make you extremely sick. Also, you are likely to build up a tolerance—if you stop using them, you crash. Reality can become unbearable and withdrawal can be agony.

Drugs that your doctor prescribes are better because their effects are more predictable. Scientists have tested them for purity and quality, established safe dosage amounts, and their side effects are known. Also, the doctor monitors your consumption to make sure the drugs are working right and that you don't take too much.

It's a bad idea to take illegal or over-the-counter drugs if you are already on antidepressants or other psychiatric medications. Combining these substances can make you very sick

Starving for Acceptance

By Anonymous

In sixth grade, I was a chubby 10-year-old. In seventh grade, I still had what was considered "baby fat" while every other girl was blooming into her preteens, or at least it seemed that way to me. Being a bit chubby usually didn't bother me. But sometimes the popular boys would say I was a fat pig who no man would ever love, and that I'd grow up to be a lonely old woman staring out the window of my apartment. I wasn't the only victim of their teasing, but since I wasn't popular, I felt alone and ugly.

I envied the girls who wore the tight pants and tank tops that showed their bellies a little. My mom wouldn't let me dress that way. Instead, I wore long-sleeved shirts with baggy pants. It's not that I wanted to wear those sexier, more revealing clothes. But I felt like all the girls in my school were perfect, beautiful swimsuit models and I was the fat ugly duckling.

The junior high prom was approaching. I saw it as the time to look grownup and beautiful. I didn't want to be the girl standing alone in the corner with everyone dancing around me.

I was tired of people teasing me, so I decided to lose weight by dieting. Around October of eighth grade, I started to eat only crackers and tuna fish with salad dressing for lunch.

soon grew tired of eating tuna every day. Before, I'd had sandwiches or hot soup for lunch. So I started to have a handful of crackers with cheese instead.

Then I got tired of that, too, and I stopped eating everything but crackers. I felt like I couldn't eat anything else for lunch or I'd never lose the weight I wanted to.

I'd never cared for breakfast because I find it too heavy a meal too early in the day. So I didn't eat breakfast. Dinner was just a small bowl of rice and some beans. I ate dinner with my mom, who usually cooked rice, beans, and some kind of meat, like pork chops or steak. She knew that I wasn't a big fan of meat so she didn't pay attention to the fact that I skipped over it and also ate less rice and beans.

I felt hungry the first weeks of my diet, and my stomach hurt a lot. I was also experiencing headaches and dizziness, and I was tired all the time. I kept wanting to eat something to make the pain go away, but I was afraid to eat and then feel too full. Feeling full made me feel fat.

After some time, I got used to the way I was feeling and began eating even less. I ate crackers every other day for lunch for four months. On the days that I didn't eat crackers, I didn't eat anything at all.

I started to lose weight, and I felt good about myself. I was getting thinner, and I knew that it wouldn't be long before all the baby fat would be gone.

While Mom didn't notice my smaller portions, she noticed I was losing weight. She just thought it was a sign of puberty and growing up. She'd comment on how I was looking slimmer because I was getting taller and becoming a "young lady."

I was pleased with my diet plan until one day, halfway through the year, a friend asked if I thought one of our classmates, who'd lost weight recently, was anorexic. I didn't know what the word *anorexic* meant, so she told me it was a person who didn't eat, just to lose weight. She also told me that anorexia is a psychological disease that kills.

That's when I realized that I might have a problem. I'd made myself think I was an overweight cow who needed to dramatically lose weight, that if I could only lose the weight, I'd be perfect.

I realized I was losing weight through self-starvation.

All of a sudden I felt like I was committing a terrible sin, like I was a witness to a horrific crime but hiding out instead of testifying in court.

I became disgusted when I realized that I was losing the weight through self-starvation. But I liked losing the weight, and I still had my goal to reach: the prom.

From September to June, I went from 125 pounds to 99 pounds. During the process of losing weight, I felt proud because I felt like I finally had control over my body fat.

I knew I looked stunning in my prom dress. But I felt like crap—physically and emotionally. I knew how I'd lost my weight. I was starving myself. I thought I was in control but I was wrong. It was unhealthy, and I knew it.

I was aware of how beautiful I looked, but I still wasn't happy with myself. I felt empty because I knew I'd never be satisfied with my appearance. I felt worthless because even after I lost the weight, people in my school still treated me like crap. Now instead of calling me "cow" or "pig," they called me "monkey." And I felt sick because I was always getting headaches and having a feeling of wanting to vomit.

I wanted to stay forever thin at 99 pounds, so when I got to high school, I continued skipping breakfast and would go to the library instead of lunch. But toward the middle of the year, I found I couldn't concentrate during 40-minute classes. I was stressed out and realized that I had to start eating something, anything, during the day to keep me energized.

So I started eating breakfast every morning—a bagel with cream cheese and chocolate milk. I would've eaten something lighter, but they don't sell light meals in my school, and I didn't have healthy food at home.

Every morning I had this breakfast and at home I ate a regular-sized plate of food with rice, meat, and beans. At the end of freshman year, I weighed 110 pounds. I liked that weight. I was only a bit heavier than I'd been in eighth grade, but I was also healthy.

Sophomore year I stopped eating breakfast again because I wanted to get to school a little later. Instead, I started to eat the school lunch. With meals like pizza, tacos, and chicken nuggets, the weight just piled on me. I was back to 125 pounds by June.

Eventually, my weight got to me again, and in January of my junior year, I cut down on my eating habits once more. I stopped buying soda every day, and I stopped eating the rice in school. At home I'd eat vegetables only or not eat anything at all. In a matter of weeks, my stomach was shrinking, I wasn't feeling hungry anymore, and I knew that I was back on the anorexia track.

When I'd lost about 7 pounds, one of my mom's friends approached me and said, "Oh, my God! You lost so much weight. You look good, though. Keep going—it'll do you good." She made me feel like I'd been a huge balloon before.

When some of my friends told me that I'd lost weight, I felt like they were worried. They'd tell me that I should eat something because I was skinny enough.

I was glad they cared about me, but mostly I felt annoyed when they tried dragging me to Wendy's. I felt that it was my body and they shouldn't tell me what to do with it or force me to eat something I didn't want to eat.

But when people didn't say anything about my weight change, I felt as though I hadn't lost enough for them to notice.

I reached 104 pounds last April. My clothes were huge on me. I liked the way I looked, but I wanted to get back to 99 pounds.

I still long to be supermodel thin. Watching the Miss America pageants, the fashion runways, and the music videos with pretty girls in cool outfits, I want to be them. I want to be able to dress in all the latest fashions like the mini-mini skirts and tube tops (not on a daily basis, just dressing up to go out somewhere), without worrying about fat flowing over the rims. I know I could tone my stomach with exercise, but I feel like I don't have time for that.

> I envied the girls who wore the tight pants.

In the past, no one told me that I was beautiful, pretty, or even attractive. All I ever heard was that I was "cute." Cute—a term I connect with children filled with baby fat.

People still call me "cute," and I hate it. But people do accept me more than in middle school. They don't tease me anymore. Maybe it has something to do with their being more mature, or the fact that I went to a different high school than most of my middle school classmates. But I also feel that it's because now I am what mainstream society wants—the perfect size.

I have more friends and an active social life. I even have a boyfriend, a boyfriend who has told me numerous times that he loves me no matter what. He knows I'm self-conscious about my body, and he helps me by telling me that I'm perfect the way I am. He also tells me, "Love is not about appearances. It's about the beauty within." He makes me feel like I don't have to lose weight to please his eye.

Sometimes it makes me wonder why I do crash diets anyway. If he loves me, then I should love myself and not worry about my weight. I know I'm the perfect size, but I'm still not content. My life isn't perfect—I'm stressed about getting into college, I'm worried about people not liking me, I'm afraid of people finding out what's wrong with me.

Don't have any control over these things, but I do have control over what I eat. I continue to not eat, but it's not an everyday thing. I usually diet, stop dieting, gain weight, get disgusted, and do the cycle over and over again.

I know that I have an eating disorder, but every time I try to control it, to eat normally, I hate the way I look and feel, so I go back to my old ways, hoping that the fat will leave my system. I know I'm damaging my body by not eating, but I feel like it's the only way for me to lose weight.

I don't want to have this constant feeling that I'm fat and need to lose weight. People look at me and say, "Damn, I didn't know you were that skinny! You should eat a hamburger!" So I know that to everyone else I am thin.

I do want a way to balance my health and appearance, but it's so hard. Sometimes I get so hungry that I just want to eat and eat and eat until I feel sick and want to throw up. But other times I don't want to even look at food because I know I'd feel sick if I ate it. I know I need to moderate the amount of food I eat but it feels too hard for me.

The pressure I once felt from my peers no longer exists. I am the only one who is forcing me to think negatively about my body. I don't want to feel this way, yet I do. I feel as if two people are pulling me in different directions and I'm being torn.

I want to be thin, but I want to be happy with myself. Yes, people have learned to accept me. Now I'm the one who has to learn how to accept myself.

The author was 17 when she wrote this story.

SHAPIN' UP!

By Antwaun Garcia

Before I went into foster care at age 9, I was slim. I was the skinniest of all my cousins. We never had much food in my house, so when I came into my foster home, I was straight. At times I couldn't stop eating. I started to gain weight, but I stayed in shape playing basketball.

At the age of 14, I began lifting weights to improve my body. I figured that to be in shape and add a little muscle wouldn't hurt me. So I began lifting about 200 pounds of free weights to build up my chest and my arms.

But when I hit about 15, I stopped playing basketball. I also started drinking nothing but soda and eating twice as much as I did before. Instead of having one sandwich, I would have two with extra mayo. When my aunt made chicken, I would eat at least a whole chicken myself. I would stay out late eating street food, the usual Chinese food, pizza, beef patties, Oreos and Doritos. I began to gain a whole lot of weight. Between ages 15 and 17, I must have gained about 150 pounds.

I didn't realize how big I was getting until I looked at pictures and saw I had a fat neck. My stomach was out there, and my thighs were as huge as Oprah's in her fat phase. I hated the way I looked, and I noticed I wasn't getting the same response from females as I did when I was slimmer. I knew I needed to think about losing weight.

Then one summer two years ago, I was with a female and she flat out told me that she was not used to dating big men. She said that, in some ways, she was embarrassed by me.

I knew I had to lose weight but her comments pushed me over the limit. I was like, "It's a wrap. It's time to train like Rocky." I went to get a routine checkup from the doctor and I weighed 291 pounds. I was pissed that I had allowed myself to get that big. The next week I began my training, harder than I ever had in my life.

I had something to prove to myself, and I wouldn't let anyone stop me from losing weight. I was going to lose it the right way, and I knew no diet would work. I wasn't messing with no pills, no drinks, or no special impossible-to-follow diet.

I started to drink more water, about five to six glasses a day. I began eating less. I still ate what I would usually eat, the same baked ziti, chicken, all that good stuff. The difference was how much I ate. I knew to eat one piece of chicken instead of the whole bird, eat mainly vegetables, and stay away from simple carbohydrates like white bread, rice, and potatoes. Instead of sucking down six pieces of Wonder bread, I would eat two pieces of wheat bread.

Before, I never ate breakfast in the morning, so when I came home to eat lunch, I would eat too much. Then I would have a big dinner and fall asleep. I couldn't do that anymore, not if I wanted to lose weight. So I would eat something for breakfast, maybe a banana and some orange juice. When I came home for lunch, I wasn't as hungry. So I would eat a tuna sandwich and drink a glass of milk and then have an apple for a snack a half hour later. That way I wouldn't be starving for dinner. At dinnertime, I would eat less meat and starch and twice as many veggies. At night if I wanted a snack, I ate crackers with a little Kool-Aid. I was good.

I also started working out again. My basic workout was shadow boxing. That's no different from boxing, but it's by yourself. I figured that boxers are some of the fittest athletes around, so why not imitate them to get in shape? I would work on the speed of my jabs and hooks.

After about fifteen minutes of boxing, I would do some sit-ups and then some push-ups. I would do no more than about twenty push-ups to start off with and about fifty sit-ups a night. I also bought a jump rope to help build my endurance and stamina. I would jump rope for at least three minutes straight.

I lost 51 pounds by working out and eating properly.

When I first started, I knew my body wouldn't be able to take long workouts like it used to. I would start off working out for only a half hour. Then, after every month, I planned to increase the time by about ten to fifteen minutes so my body could get adjusted to it. I also knew working out solo would be boring, so I added some music to my routine. Also, I went back to playing basketball.

Sometimes when I trained, I thought about that comment my girl said to me, that I was too big for her. Then I would think, "Who cares what she says, this is about my health and if I don't give a damn about it, then who will?"

I worked out the whole winter. When Thanksgiving and Christmas came around, I ate whatever I wanted, but that next morning, I worked all the turkey, chicken, and cakes off.

From December 12 to the end of February, I worked out continually. When March hit, the results of my work were visible. People were like, "Antwaun! Oh my God, you lost so much weight!"

At first I didn't pay no mind to it. I thought they were saying it to say it. Then more and more people told me that I had lost weight. My teachers in my school, my grandparents, my aunt, my cousins, and even the girl who was embarrassed by me. She was all on me, like, "You look so good. I'm so proud of you."

I was thinking, "I didn't do this for you! I did this for myself." But it was true. I'd lost a lot of weight. I was able to wear tank tops, and they fit me properly. I could fit into my old jerseys and sweaters. When I got back on the scale that March, I weighed 240.

I had lost fifty-one pounds in three months. I did all that with no fad diet, no pills, just a lot of working out and eating properly.

I began wearing brighter colors because I looked right in them. I wore more white, more red, gray, and blue. I took pics wherever I went, and I noticed the difference in my appearance. I still feel I have some weight to lose. Now I am 235 pounds, and I am 6'1", so I don't want to lose more than 20 or 30 pounds. But I think a solid 200 to 215 pounds would fit me fine. I want to keep in shape, maybe build a little six-pack, and some muscular arms.

But for now, I'm also happy with what I've accomplished. It felt good to lose weight, and it felt good to set a goal and stick to it.

Antwaun was 19 when he wrote this story.

ADDLED ON ADDERALL

By Anonymous

My dad thinks that, because the private school I attend is so expensive, he should get the results that he's paying for. When either my brother or I falter, he blows up.

Once, in seventh grade, what started as a dinner conversation about what I could do to pull up my grades ended with my dad shouting at me for being lazy and not working hard enough. When he said those things to me, I felt like a loser and a disappointment. I also felt guilty that I was wasting his money.

I resolved to try harder in school and prove to my dad that I cared about his sacrifices. This, along with my own personal desire to do well and a school environment where my friends whined over getting a B+, made me feel an immense pressure to succeed. I developed a competitive side that was fueled by insecurity and anxiety about not being as smart or hard-working as my peers.

Daily Stress
By the time I was a high school freshman, my anxiety—and my schedule—was out of control. A typical day went something like this: Wake up at 7 a.m. and grab a Red Bull to drink on my way to school. In class, I remind myself to raise my

hand and force myself to concentrate. I solve an equation in Algebra 2, but I have the wrong answer, and my face flushes red with embarrassment as some other girl raises her hand and flawlessly corrects the mistake. Time for English, where I try hard to say something that will make my teacher exclaim, "Brilliant!" I fail.

Walking to lunch, I hear a junior complaining about the SATs, which sends a wave of panic through me. Now lunch. Tara's mad at Samantha for some reason and wants me to agree with her that Sam's a bitch. Then Sam pulls me aside and tries to convince me that Tara's a bitch. Truth is, I don't really care. Before I've eaten half my grilled cheese, the bell rings and my half hour lunch break is over. It's time for more tests, more hurdles for me to jump over, more chances for me to prove myself, though I never quite feel like I'm doing anything right.

The stress doesn't end after school. I need to write articles for the school paper or volunteer at a homeless shelter or design a layout for the yearbook. I feel an intense need to get into an amazing, impressive college, and in order to do that, I think I have to do a ridiculous amount of extracurriculars. Almost all of the kids at my school go on to top colleges; in fact, the whole point of my school is prepare us to get into top colleges.

I finally get home at 7 p.m., watch TV while snacking, then take a nap until 10:30. I miss dinner, but I've filled up on Pringles so it doesn't matter. I wake up panicked, remembering the massive stack of homework I have sitting on my desk; I down another Red Bull to get motivated. Whenever I encounter a difficult math problem or English question, I have a moment of panic. I worry that my answer will be wrong, so instead of giving it a shot, I procrastinate and focus on Facebook.

Finally, at 1:30 a.m., I collapse into bed, not quite ready to resume the routine in just five and a half hours. I'm still wired from the Red Bull, so I toss and turn, thinking about how something in this routine has to change.

I should have tried to increase my energy by getting to sleep earlier, eating healthier, limiting my extra-curriculars, and cutting down on Facebook. I did all of these things eventually. But back then, none of these ideas occurred to me. Maybe I didn't think I was capable of making these changes on my own. Instead, I found the answer in a pill.

A Capsule of Focus
One day, I was surfing the internet instead of studying for a biology test, when I read an article about how college students were using the prescription drug Adderall, usually prescribed to people with ADHD (Attention Deficit Hyperactivity Disorder), to get ahead. According to the students interviewed, the drug allowed them to concentrate better, and gave them enough energy to stay up late studying for hours at a time.

Even though the article listed the dangers of using Adderall without a prescription—irregular heartbeat, dangerously high body temperatures, potential for heart failure or seizures, feelings of hostility or paranoia—I was fascinated by the idea that a drug could help someone do better in school.

In my mind, I was way behind my peers and needed all the help I could possibly get. I was sick of feeling inadequate, sick of getting the wrong answer in math class and never feeling like I was working hard enough. My insecurities had been building during the first months of freshman year, and I would do almost anything to get rid of them. After watching another documentary about Adderall on YouTube, I knew I wanted to get my hands on it. But how?

I had my own blog on the website Tumblr, where I posted pictures, videos and quotes that I liked. None of my friends had Tumblr blogs but me, so I felt that I could express myself freely. However, the blog is also public, and lots of other people use Tumblr.

An idea occurred to me. What if I created a post asking if there was anyone who lived in New York City who would sell me Adderall? I didn't have my name anywhere on my blog, so I figured I couldn't get in trouble for it. I impulsively created the post, then hit "publish."

Drug Deal at Barnes & Noble
The next day, a girl named Sarah replied, telling me that she had access to the drug. I was terrified to meet up with a stranger, but her blog gave the impression that she was a normal high school kid in need of some money. I knew she could have been lying and that she might not be who she said she was. And, of course, purchasing Adderall without a prescription is illegal. Though I was vaguely aware of these dangers at the time, I was so focused on trying to get ahead that my better judgment was obscured.

We planned to meet at the Union Square Barnes &Noble after school. While going down the escalator, we made the trade-off: 4 pills for $20, one week of my allowance. During the cab ride home, I popped in one of the pills, $5 gone in an instant. I wasn't sure what to expect, but once I got home and started my homework, I felt the effect quickly.

I started my homework at 5 p.m. The next time I looked up at the clock, it was 8:30. I had focused on my homework, without a break in concentration, for three and a half hours. I'd never done that before. I was starting to feel good and very energized, like I could do anything I put my mind to, so I decided to get ahead on the week's work. By the time I had finished all of my history reading for the week, I realized that I had forgotten all about dinner, but I wasn't even hungry. I felt superhuman.

After spending an hour cleaning and organizing my room, which was unusual for me, I headed to bed around 1:30 a.m. I was still keyed up. I'm a naturally anxious person and the Adderall intensified my anxiety; I spent four hours worrying about almost every aspect of my life before I finally fell asleep.

A Magic Pill?
The next morning, after just two hours of sleep, I was completely exhausted, foggy, and grumpy. After pulling myself out of bed, I remembered that I had Adderall, my secret power. I took another one of my pills, $5 gone, and pretty soon felt almost as energized as I did the night before. And thus the cycle began.

Despite the side effects, as the week wore on, I came to the conclusion that Adderall was the solution to all my problems. I could concentrate for hours, my mind felt sharper, and I felt more energized than ever. I realized, though, that at this rate, four pills wouldn't cut it. I had about $400 saved up in my bank account from birthday and holiday presents, and that kept me going for a while. I was getting my homework done at record speeds, meeting with Sarah to replenish my stash about once a week, and I felt good.

My friends, however, started to notice that I was acting weird. Whenever we'd talk, I would always gear the conversation towards school and homework, which got old after a while. I'd always ask them what grades they got on papers and quizzes and tests so I could compare myself to them. They didn't like how competitive and obsessive about schoolwork I was becoming.

I hardly had fun when I was hanging out with them, either. Because the Adderall amplified my anxiety, it caused me to ceaselessly compare myself to my friends, and kept me from letting loose or joking around them. On Adderall, I wasn't really capable of having fun.

Though, at the time, I felt like Adderall was helping my school work, it was actually hurting it in unforeseen ways. Because Adderall sped me up, I lost the ability to thoroughly analyze my work. I didn't take the time to edit and perfect my essays, and I often made careless mistakes in math and science.

One English essay I wrote when I was on Adderall was returned to me without a grade. I met with my English teacher, who said it wasn't up to my usual standard, but mercifully gave me a B. He said that, while my paper had a lot of interesting ideas about the novel we were reading, the writing style was sloppy, repetitive, and unpolished. I had turned it in without proofreading it, and it was riddled with typos and grammatical mistakes.

I was also developing a resistance to Adderall, so I was using increasingly more of it to get the same effect. This was draining the money that I had carefully saved through the years. Worse, I was feeling dependent on it. In order to feel powerful and intelligent, I had to take the drug. When I wasn't taking it, I felt sloppy and lazy. The longer this went on, the worse I felt about using it. I wasn't proud of my work, or myself.

A Dangerous Combo

All of this culminated at my friend Maggie's party, about three weeks after I started taking Adderall. It was one of my first real high school parties, and my friends and I had been looking forward to it all month, carefully planning the guest list, making a playlist of good dance music, and cleaning her basement to be a party space.

People started arriving, and all of my friends were having fun, mingling and flirting with guys. But I couldn't lose the intense anxiety brimming in me. I had taken a pill earlier in the day and it hadn't worn off yet. My usual anxiety over schoolwork was now translated into social anxiety. I was scared that no one would talk to me or that I would embarrass myself. I am usually a bit nervous during big social situations, but it usually goes away quickly. This time, it wouldn't go away.

In order to calm my nerves, I drank some of the Mike's Hard Lemonade that Maggie's friend bought with a fake ID, but it only made me feel worse. Because Adderall severely reduced my appetite, I hadn't eaten anything in a while and so the alcohol hit me stronger than I expected.

Adderall can hinder your ability to tell whether or not you're too tired or intoxicated, so while on Adderall, you can end up drinking more than you're used to. Although your mind might not recognize that you are drinking too much, your body is feeling the effect of the alcohol. This may have happened to me that night, because I started to feel very sick, even though I didn't think that I drank too much. I was feeling so ill that I left the party extremely early, without saying goodbye to my friends.

Cut Off
I didn't like how Adderall was crippling my social life, and it scared me how anxious I was becoming. I was sick of never getting a good night's sleep, and going through my days feeling like an anxious, work-obsessed zombie. Plus, I could tell my mom was beginning to get suspicious about how often I was asking her for money.

I pushed my doubts away, though. I decided that I would have to sacrifice my emotional well being and my social life in order to succeed academically. I would continue to take the drug. It wasn't completely up to me, though.

About a week after the party, I was sitting in assembly, fiddling with my cell phone when I got a text from Sarah. I almost had a heart attack when I read it. She said that she couldn't sell me Adderall anymore because her little brother, from whom she was getting the Adderall to sell, was being taken off the drug.

I knew she was lying. When I saw her a week earlier, she had seemed concerned about me. When I told her I wanted 10 pills, she said, "Are you sure you want that many? Don't take too much . . ." as she giggled nervously. I could tell she was having doubts about selling to me, and didn't want to be responsible if something bad happened.

Now, I'm really grateful that she decided to stop, but at the time, I was pissed off. I texted her desperately, asking if she had any other hookups and to stop lying, but she wouldn't change her mind and eventually stopped replying. I got in trouble for texting during assembly, but I didn't care. I was on my last pill.

Changing My Habits

That week was difficult. Without the pills, I felt tired, irritable, hungry, and lazy. But these feelings went away within a few days and I began to feel more like my old self. I felt almost like I was waking up from a dream. I realized, though, that if I wanted to succeed without drugs, I had to make some kind of permanent change.

I decided to start small. I began to use my free periods to do homework instead of socialize, so I'd have more time to relax when I got home. I stopped napping after school, since I would always wake up groggy and not in the mood for homework. I set aside some time after school to use Facebook and socialize with my friends, but I closed social networking sites when I was trying to do homework.

These changes had a big impact on me, because they allowed me to complete my homework at an earlier hour, really concentrate while I was doing it, and get a better night's sleep. I found that, when I was more rested, I could focus more in class, and my mind felt clearer. I even felt happier when I got more sleep.

These small changes added up, and pretty soon, my Bs became A-minuses. This success made me feel more confident, and I began to trust myself more. The confidence made me feel more comfortable asking questions in class. At first, asking questions for me was difficult and my heart pounded when I raised my hand, but eventually it got easier and easier. Asking questions helped me better understand what I was missing before, and improved my academic performance as well.

I Won't Throw It All Away

I finished my freshman year with a good, but not perfect, academic record. I was proud that I had finally learned to adapt to high school life. However, my insecurity didn't entirely vanish after my freshman year. It still pops up, and I have to make sure I manage it in a healthy way.

Right before midterms in my sophomore year, I didn't do well on a geometry test that I had studied for. I was crushed, and thought about turning to Adderall again. After all, I reasoned, it was going to be midterms, and everyone does Adderall during exam season, right? A lot of the older kids at my school talked about it, so it couldn't be that bad.

I went on another website, where there was a forum called "Adderall NYC." I contacted a complete stranger, username Undercover Dolphin, about buying Adderall. We set up a time and a place to meet, but in the end I decided not to go.

I thought about all the progress I had made since freshman year, and reminded myself of the dangers of turning back to the drug. I reminded myself that just because I didn't do well on one test doesn't mean I couldn't handle midterms. Before, I would compare myself to everyone else and wonder why I was so bad at geometry. This time, I pumped myself up and focused on doing the best that I could.

I finished the year with almost an A average. Even though my parents and teachers are proud of me, what matters most is that I am proud of myself, and that I earned those grades using my own capabilities.

PART TWO:

THE FOUNDATION OF HEALTH:
EATING RIGHT

DEAR FOOD DIARY:

What We Learned from Recording Every Bite

As part of our writing about food and nutrition, several writers kept food diaries, recording every bite (and sip) for four long weeks. Along the way, our writers made some surprising discoveries about themselves and their diets. At the end of the month, nutritionist Kristen Mancinelli evaluated the diaries and counseled the group on how they could improve their eating habits.

Don't Drink Your Calories
Suzy Berkowitz

Looking at my diary entries, I realized my food intake consisted largely of dairy and carbohydrates, with very few fruits or vegetables. On the other hand, though my solid-food diet was pretty unhealthy, I must credit myself for drinking wisely. Almost all the liquid I consume is either water or seltzer, two drinks that the nutritionist we spoke to recommended highly. She told us that high-calorie drinks may be more responsible for the obesity epidemic than high-calorie foods.

For me, wasting my calorie and sugar allowance on drinks was never an issue; I rarely drank soda as a kid, and I don't usually crave it. I also realized at a young age that juice isn't as healthy as many people believe. Fruit juices don't contain fiber, and fiber is an important ingredient in solid fruits. Fiber can't be digested, but its presence in foods helps you feel full and metabolize the sugar in fruit. By drinking a liquid form of fruit without fiber, you end up consuming more sugar than you should. (The ideal serving of juice is only four ounces, but many "individual" bottles contain three or more times that amount!)

By replacing fruit juices with actual fruits, and drinking water or seltzer, you'll consume less sugar. You may even find that more fiber in your diet curbs your appetite.

Junking Junk Food—Without Going Hungry
By Mohammed Hussain

I've always promised to lay off junk food for a week, but when I stare at the Doritos bag or that tray of Oreo cookies, my resolve never lasts. Since I'm so skinny, my concept of being healthy means eating more to gain weight. And because of its accessibility, junk food has played a large role in my "eat more to be healthy" regime.

But I know that eating to gain weight isn't the same as eating healthily. So I decided to volunteer for a one-week, no-junkfood diet. This time, I knew I would stick to my plan: since I'd be reporting on my diet experiment for this issue, I finally had a concrete reason not to indulge.

Letting go, however, still proved difficult. Usually, I have milk and pound cake for breakfast. During the no-junk-food week, I had only milk. It didn't fill me up, but I didn't consider eating anything else. I believed that cutting out junk was enough to constitute a healthy diet.

During the week, lunch consisted of a Caesar salad from McDonald's with lettuce, ranch dressing, croutons, and tomatoes. The salad was a healthier alternative than the pizza I usually had, but I didn't enjoy it because I don't like tomatoes, and in general, it wasn't satisfying. At lunchtime on the second day of the diet, I was close to buying pizza and only resisted because the other writers threatened to tell my editors on me.

In my household, we eat traditional dinners, which mainly consist of rice with other foods. For the no-junk-food diet, my dinner meals remained largely the same: sometimes I ate rice with chicken, other times with spinach, fish, lettuce, or beans.

On Friday, Saturday, and Sunday of the diet week, since the workshop wasn't open, I had more time for breakfast. So, in addition to milk, I ate fruits like cherries and strawberries—something I rarely do for breakfast on a typical day. I had no lunch during these days, because I decided that I didn't want to travel to my local McDonald's for another salad. I couldn't think of any lunch that wouldn't be junk food and would seem like a real meal. I had dinner early those days.

The week after my diet ended, we met with the nutritionist. Ironically, she told me I'd failed to eat healthily even while on a no-junk-food diet. For starters, I was consuming too few calories. Drinking only milk for breakfast was a bad idea, because it neither satisfied me nor included a mixture of food groups. Instead, I should have supplemented the milk with fruits, like I did during the non-workshop days, and some sort of high-fiber, low-sugar carbohydrate, like oatmeal or whole wheat toast.

Furthermore, skipping lunch on Friday, Saturday, and Sunday was also an unhealthy choice. Instead of getting a salad with little protein and lots of high-fat dressing, I could've gone to my local deli for a whole wheat bagel with cream cheese and maybe some yogurt, another piece of fruit, or some veggies.

Clearly, eating healthy doesn't need to mean having a bad time. I was eating foods that I didn't like, but after talking to Kristen, I realized that oatmeal, peanuts, carrots, and whole wheat toast are all healthy foods that I actually enjoy. Also, by making sure I eat some protein and unsaturated fat—foods like avocadoes, nuts, and lean meats—along with several servings of whole fruits and vegetables each day, I don't need to feel hungry while eating well.

If I'd used my diet as a chance to explore healthy foods, it would've been more fun and I would've had more energy. Completely eliminating junk food from one's diet isn't easy, but adding more good food is easier than I thought.

Size Matters
By Parameshwari Maragatham

When I started my food diary, I hoped it would give me some insight into why my weight fluctuates. Though I'm portly, I tend to eat a balanced diet, abundant with vegetables, fruits, and protein. I can't say I don't adore potato chips, cheese curls, and Chinese takeout, but I eat them much less than I do my mom's homemade meals.

There's something important to note about those meals: Besides the weekly frittata and occasional pasta or salad, most of my mother's cooking is what she was fed while she was growing up in India. Thus, I will eat potato masala, a traditional Indian dish made with vegetables and spices, before I eat French fries.

Look to the cuisine of your parents or ancestors and you'll probably find something that's healthy as well as delicious. Traditional cuisines are made with fresh, whole ingredients. I usually eat sambhar for dinner, which is a soup made from yellow lentils, garlic, ginger, black pepper, and vegetables, along with many spices: cilantro, coriander, cumin, asafoetida, and mustard seeds. Traditionally, sambhar is eaten with a rice product, but I like it best on its own. It has a hearty taste since it's been simmering all day, and it's wholesome, thick, and savory.

Alongside the good news my food diary showed me, though, there was a bit of bad news. I usually overeat by at least a portion size, especially when I go out to eat. This is a problem even when you're eating healthy food.

The nutritionist who reviewed our food diaries gave me specific advice about portion size. She suggested I take a single serving and eat at a slow pace, chewing thoroughly and enjoying each mouthful as if it were my last for that meal. When I'm halfway done with my portion, I should check in with myself to see if I'm still hungry. If I am, I can keep eating. If I'm still hungry after finishing that first portion, then I can get a second portion—but if I'm no longer hungry, I should stop.

Although it's hard to let go of my entrenched habits, knowing just how much I eat will make me more aware of how food is affecting my waistline and I'll be more inclined to change my habits.

Follow Your Appetite, Not the Crowd
By Chantal Hylton

When I started my food journal, I was ashamed to write down what I normally ate. I wanted to manipulate the end result so my journal reflected a healthy diet. To do that, I only ate salads and drank water for our first week. That didn't last long.

By the second week, I found myself falling back into my old habits of Chinese takeout and fast food every day. At the end of each day, I was tempted to lie about what I had eaten, not only because it seemed unhealthy, but also because I was disgusted with it. I didn't want to add those two extra cheeseburgers to my food diary. But I was honest and soon my journal seemed like a book of overindulgence.

As I wrote my journal entries I discovered something else: I wasn't eating to give my body nourishment, but to help me blend into social settings. I ate food I didn't want because someone brought it home for me. I also ate because I was out with friends and I didn't want to be the only person without a plate in front of me. There were times when I wasn't hungry, but I found myself unconsciously reaching over for a friend's fries. I only noticed this because I had to write it down. I was always hanging out with friends and family, and my food journal helped me to see that I was just eating what they ate, not letting my own appetite lead me.

I made a conscious effort to change my eating habits. My food journal haunted me, and every time I shared a meal with someone I thought, "If I eat this I am going to have to write it down in my food journal. Am I actually hungry or am I just eating to blend in?" I also started eating healthier foods, which became easier to do the more I learned about a balanced diet.

I stopped writing in my journal the first chance I got, but my new, healthier eating habits are still in place. I didn't need to overhaul my whole diet, as I feared when I began. I just needed to do a little repair. Mostly, I needed to make sure that I eat because I'm actually hungry, not just because I'm around other people who are eating.

Detecting the Fakes (and Flakes)
By Annmarie Turton

Keeping a food journal helped me spot the "fake" healthy foods in my diet. My usual breakfast consists of Raisin Bran with milk and a cup of tea. After writing it down day after day in my journal, I started wondering how healthy it really is and decided to read the label on the back of the cereal box. I was surprised to see that two main ingredients were sweeteners:

sugar and high-fructose corn syrup, which are both high in calories but have no nutritional value.

We grow up thinking that cereal is healthy because it's made from grains and has lots of health claims on the box. But when a nutritionist reviewed our journals, she recommended that we not eat cereal at all, which surprised all of us. She explained that the flakes in most cereals have gone through a refining process that strips the grain of nutrients and fiber. Later, nutritional additives are baked in to make the cereal appear healthier—but we'd be better off eating oatmeal, which isn't refined in the first place. Another bad thing about many cereals is that they are loaded with sugar. In fact, half the weight of some cereals is just sugar. Examples of sugar-loaded cereals are Trix, Cap'n Crunch, Apple Jacks, and Corn Pops. (There are a few good cereals, Kristen said, that have little or no sugar and are made from whole grains, like unfrosted Shredded Wheat and Grape-Nuts.)

Most teens—like me—find it almost impossible to wean ourselves off cereal. But we can make small changes to find more balance in our diets. For example, we can reduce the amount of cereal in our bowls and add fruits such as blueberries or bananas. Then we'll be getting a good dose of grain, fiber, and fruit.

You Don't Have to Be Wealthy to Eat Healthy
By Jaminson Robinson

When I was first handed a composition notebook and told to record everything I ate, I thought, "No problem." I believed I ate healthy most of the time. Over the next four weeks my food diary proved me wrong.

After the first week, I started to realize that my diet mainly consisted of just meat—in other words, protein, which we're advised to consume in relatively small quantities. I also realized I wasn't consuming many fruits or vegetables, which we're supposed to eat in abundance.

Like a lot of the other NYC writers, I thought eating healthier would mean spending more money. I started adding it up: Four days a week for two weeks straight, I had bought a ham and cheese sandwich on a hero (with a little lettuce, tomato, and mustard), cranberry juice, and a banana at a local deli for lunch. It cost eight dollars in total, which meant I spent $64 just on lunch over two weeks. I thought this was fairly healthy and not too expensive.

However, after talking to the nutritionist, I realized that I could have had a healthier lunch for less money if I'd been willing to do a little more work. I could have bought healthier bread, like high-fiber whole wheat, at a nearby grocery store, along with ham and cheese. I could have easily added lettuce, tomatoes, and mustard from home. If I made my own sandwich, I could even ensure that the sandwich was packed with more veggies (spinach or green peppers, even) and a little less ham and cheese than a typical deli sandwich. I could also buy cheaper fruit at a local fruit stand and simply drink tap water instead of high-calorie juice. Certainly I would have spent less than $64 if I'd made these healthy adjustments.

I realized that it really takes thought and effort to eat healthy. It's not enough to pick out a few things that you think may be healthy; you really have to take into consideration the balance of food groups, make an effort to find out what is actually in your food (look at labels!), and work a bit harder to create your own healthy meals.

GLUTTONY GETAWAY

By Elsa Ho

"OK, let's double check to make sure we got everything we need: Oreos, Cool Ranch Doritos, Sweet and Spicy Doritos, two packets of chicken meat, Cookies and Cream ice cream, Gatorade, gummy worms, hot chocolate mix, broccoli, bacon, and sausage."

We put everything on the cashier's counter, thinking this was all we needed for the rest of our stay at the resort. We would soon discover how it felt to survive on junk food for more than a day. This happened last spring break, when five of my friends and I took a vacation at a self-catering resort in the Pocono Mountains with no adult supervision. We did the laundry, washed the dishes, went grocery shopping, and—most importantly—cooked for ourselves.

On the first night, we were eager to make our dinner because, for most of us, cooking was a new, fresh experience. It was like playing kitchen in elementary school. We took out all the utensils from the cabinets and laid out all the food in front of us.

Once we laid the groceries out, we noticed something about the pile. Out of all the supplies we'd bought, we had only two nutritious items: chicken and broccoli. I guess we thought that was enough proper food for a dinner meal. But other than those items, we'd bought only junk.

Like my friends, I didn't think this was a major problem. As long as we had our chips, ice cream, and candy, everything was fine. So, while the only two people who knew how to work a stove cooked, the rest of us hopped onto the sofa, turned on the TV, and ferociously munched on Doritos and gummy worms. Our parents would never allow us to eat junk food right before dinner, but since there were no parents in the house, we did as we pleased.

> **We ferociously munched on Doritos and gummy worms.**

That night we ate the very first meal any of us had ever prepared. It consisted of overcooked chicken and very hard broccoli. But no one teased the amateur chefs, because we knew none of us could cook any better. We started the next morning off with a breakfast filled with calories and saturated fat. We consumed almost all the bacon, sausage, and hot chocolate. Then we went paintballing for about an hour, and after that, we were starving. We headed back to the resort but found ourselves too bruised and sore to go out for lunch. So, like the lazy teenagers we are, we ate what was most convenient: the leftover Doritos, ice cream, and some more sausage.

That night, we were faced with a problem: We'd calculated incorrectly and didn't have enough chicken for our second night's dinner. Worse, it was 11 p.m. before we even thought about dinner, so it was too late to go out to eat. And we didn't want to have food delivered, because the resort was extremely secluded and we were afraid the deliveryman would be a crazy killer with a thirst for murdering teenagers.

Our only option was to stay in the house. "Let's just finish the chicken and eat ice cream," someone suggested. We figured it wouldn't take much to fill us up, since we'd been eating chips all day.

But after finishing dinner that night, all of us realized what a horrible mistake it was not to buy some fruit and vegetables.

Within those two days, I had three meals of junk food and only one proper dinner with meat and vegetables. After those three unhealthy meals, my friends and I felt awful. Not only was the junk food not satisfying, but we felt the effects of the fat and grease from the food. We all felt sluggish, bloated, nauseated, and completely lethargic. We yearned for some apples and salad.

We all felt sluggish, bloated, nauseated, and completely lethargic.

On the third day, none of us could take it anymore. We had to call for a cab to go back to Wal-Mart and buy bananas, apples, lettuce, tomatoes, carrots, and grapes. We were all craving something healthy by that time, so the first few bites of fruit were very refreshing. The feeling was even better than eating flavorful chips and soft ice cream.

When I'm at home my mom prepares all my meals, so I'd never really thought about the effort it takes to maintain a balanced diet. My mom is like my nutritionist. She's always telling me how much work she puts into dinner to make sure that I have all the nutrients I need to remain healthy.

Every day she prepares some kind of meat, vegetables, rice, and soup, and there is always fruit in the refrigerator. She constantly worries about how my eating habits will impact my health once I leave for college. I tell her not to worry because I know how to make a few simple dishes.

But the truth is that, until our spring break trip, I never realized how vital it is to eat nutritiously. We learn about the food pyramid in school, but we never really pay attention to it.

In the Poconos, I discovered that it is essential to consume different foods and get a mixture of carbohydrates and proteins while limiting your intake of fat, sugar, and salt. Relying on junk food will eventually lead to illness. It will weigh you down, mentally and physically.

I also never realized how much effort and thought it takes to eat healthily. By the end of the trip, my friends and I yearned for a home-cooked meal prepared the right way. I'm pretty sure everyone went home that day and gobbled up everything our moms cooked.

Although I tell my mom not to worry about me when I move away from home this fall, I know that I will probably be too lazy to cook for myself and eat properly every day. But I hope at least to steer clear of junk food meals. After my unhealthy vacation, I learned that not caring what I eat will leave me feeling ill.

Elsa was 17 when she wrote this story. She later graduated from high school and went to college.

I Desperately Needed Cooking 101

By Hattie Rice

Last spring, I went to see a movie called *Super-Size Me*, about a guy who had the nerve to down Mickey D's three times a day for thirty days. (I know you're thinking he must have been one big mama jamma after that, and believe me, he was.)

The movie explained that obesity is a growing epidemic. America is the fattest nation, and a lot of it is because of fast food. The guy in Super Size Me, Morgan Spurlock, started off as a very healthy American (he exercised and ate his vegetables), but after a month of burgers and fries he was at risk of obesity and diabetes and couldn't even perform in bed. (Who would think a Big Mac could turn you into a little mac where it counts?)

This summer I joined a nutrition workshop. We learned about substitutes for the greasy food we buy (like eating baked instead of fried foods) and spent a week eating only healthy foods. The workshop provided good information, but it didn't have such a profound effect on me that I decided to dramatically change my eating habits. I do limit my intake, though, and exercise at night. We also learned to look at the nutrition facts on the back of foods. (Unless your city passes a law like New York did, you will never see a Big Mac with that information on the back, but just eat at Subway—they blow up both Burger King's and McDonald's spot.) If you do indulge in Mickey D's, you better hope that meal holds you down because those are all the calories you need for the day.

In the group, a chef helped us prepare a few healthy meals. We made Chinese stir-fry and it was slamming. It seemed easy enough. Just put olive oil in the pan at a low simmer and slowly add vegetables: mushrooms, baby corn, etc. Then we put in the noodles with some black bean sauce and soy sauce and mixed it. It seemed easy. With a chef telling us what to do, it came out perfect.

> I needed a piece of cake to calm me down.

When I dug in, I felt a little shaky, but the more of the yummy food I ate the more convinced I became that I was ready to take on cooking on my own. I was excited to test my skills. Little did I know what would happen once I got my hands on those noodles.

In fact, my healthy week went absolutely hor-ri-ble. For breakfast I had oatmeal with vanilla soy milk. It looked like caramel and tasted exactly the way a Newport smells. For lunch I had turkey and Swiss cheese (nice, right?) on wheat bread, which killed it. For dinner I had baked chicken with vegetables.

The whole time I felt like an insomniac crackhead: overly energetic and hyperactive. I found myself walking around the house for no reason. During some meals I felt insatiable, as if I had a big hole that the sun could fit through. The brownies I had for snack were just like an appetizer. I was thinking, "Bring on the cheese Danish." I needed a piece of cake to fill me up and calm me down.

Some of the food I cooked had me feeling as if I was on Fear Factor. One night I took out a frying pan and poured some olive oil in, along with some vegetables. I went to watch TV and forgot about my food until the alarm rang off. My boiling water for the noodles ended up evaporating.

The brown rice noodles (no, I'm not bugging, it was brown spaghetti) looked and tasted like straight up cardboard (that couldn't possibly have been because I was AWOL while I was supposed to be cooking). I guess I left it on too long.

My baby corn also came out looking like baby dinosaurs since I put my specialty midnight black color on them (I burned those too). The salad looked like I could have pulled leaves off a tree and it would have tasted better.

I admit that the healthy food didn't exactly cause my problems— my cooking skills, or lack of them, did.

> The salad looked like I pulled leaves off a tree.

If you can't cook and would like to avoid the heartache and pain I went through, you may turn to the Mickey D's health hazard. Don't. As *Super Size Me* showed, it's not healthy. Maybe grilled noodles and charcoal vegetables are not as bad as an extra 25 pounds.

Think about it, for every Big Mac you can have a veggie burger and a smaller waist. You'll be a few inches closer to the Brad Pitt of your and my dreams. So say "Love and Peace" to the fries with too much grease.

If you prefer to stick to your regular diet, just limit your portions, 'cause it's not what you eat, it's how much. After the workshop, I decided to limit how much I eat, and I've lost some weight. Now my only problem is, where am I going to get the money for new clothes? (You know I got to stay fresh.)

And if your cooking skills are totally inadequate like mine, it's time to find a school that has cooking 101 and sign up immediately. Even brown rice spaghetti ain't nasty. It all depends on how it's prepared. Now's the time to get off your rear end and learn to cook, because when you're on your own, nobody's going to burn the grilled cheese for you.

Hattie was 17 when she wrote this story. She graduated from high school and went to college in upstate New York.

WHY IS BAD FOOD SO GOOD?

By Chantal Hylton

As a child, I loved eating home-cooked meals—until my grand-mother introduced me to the McDonald's Kids Meal. Every time she visited, she brought a bag of McDonald's. At first, I was more interested in the toy that came with it, but eventually McDonald's became the only food I would consume. Even when I wasn't hungry, I couldn't say no to the number two meal: two cheeseburgers, French fries, and a soda.

While I was getting hooked on fast food, so was the rest of America. As a result, the obesity rate is higher than ever, and we're paying for our overeating and junk food addiction with diabetes, heart disease, and other illnesses. But even with a new weight loss book, diet plan, or miracle pill out every week, it seems that we just can't break the habit. We all won-der: Why does bad food taste so addictively good? And why can't we stop eating it? In his book, *The End of Overeating*, Dr. David A. Kessler answers those questions.

Kessler, a former commissioner of the U.S. Food and Drug Administration, explains that it was rare to find foods high in sugar, fat, or salt throughout most of evolution, so humans developed a strong craving for those things. (Nowadays, we tend to think of sugar, fat, and salt as all bad, but they are a necessary part of any diet—in small amounts.) Today, the food industry exploits those cravings.

Kessler interviews established experts in the food industry, who reveal that most packaged and restaurant food is engineered to get us hooked. Sugar, fat, and salt are the main ingredients in many food products because the food industry knows those flavors will leave us longing for more. And buying more.

The food industry even finds ways to make natural foods artificially addictive. For instance, "The White Chocolate Mocha Frappuccino served at Starbucks is coffee diluted with a mix of sugar, fat, and salt," Kessler writes. Why? Because sugar, fat, and salt increase stimulation and trigger feelings of being rewarded, leaving us eating (or drinking) long after we are full.

I had never thought about the origin of my fast-food addiction before, but Kessler's explanation made perfect sense. I definitely considered a Kids Meal to be a treat, even after the once-a-week indulgence turned into an everyday routine. As I grew older, the feeling of being rewarded every time I ate fast food never went away. That rewarding feeling, Kessler says, is what triggers overeating in many of us.

I've taught my 2-year-old sister my bad eating habits. Whenever I go visit her, I have a McDonald's bag in hand. It makes her happy. However, after reading this book, I realize that the rewarding feeling my sister and I get from fast food is just the food industry toying with our minds and bodies.

> Most packaged and restaurant food is engineered to get us hooked.

The End of Overeating scared me healthy. After reading it, I wiped my hands clean of fast food. It was a lot easier to say no once I knew what was really in it. As Kessler puts it,

"I liked McDonald's Southern Style Chicken Breast—at least until I read the ingredients list, which included sugar, salt, modified tapioca starch, maltodextrin, and artificial flavors, even before it was battered, breaded, and fried."

I wouldn't be willing to put drugs into my body or my sister's, so I am not going to feed us chemically engineered food, either. The next time my sister asks me to take her to McDonald's, I'll simply tell her, "No, it's bad for you."

Chantal was in high school when she wrote this story.

Why Should Teens Care About Nutrition?

By Stephanie Hinkson

I know it's important for us to eat well to stay healthy—and alert in school. For example, I eat Grape-Nuts for breakfast every morning because I know it's a good source of fiber. To find out more about teens' nutrition needs, I talked to Marcia A. Thomas, the coordinator of the community public health program at New York University's Department of Nutrition, Food Studies and Public Health.

Q: What do you say to teens who don't care about nutrition?
Marcia A. Thomas: Being a teenager, you're starting to make your own decisions. Teenagers need to think of health as one of those decisions.

Even though you may not see the direct relationship between what you eat and your health immediately, it really does affect you twenty years from now. And if you get used to eating a lot of junk food, a lot of sweets, drinking a lot of sodas now, it's very likely that you'll be doing that as an adult, too, because it's hard to break those habits.

But that doesn't mean you have to eat carrots and celery every day. You can still enjoy the foods that you love. It's really about balancing—you want to balance the healthy foods with the less healthy. It doesn't mean you can't ever eat cookies. It just means you should eat fewer cookies and more fruits and vegetables.

And you'll feel better if you eat well. Proper nutrition helps with mood. It helps with academic performance. Studies show a link between eating a proper diet—especially eating breakfast in the morning—and better performance in school.

Q: Why do we crave foods that are considered "junk food"?
Thomas: A lot of junk food is made of two important things that our bodies love: sugar and fat. They taste good, make us feel good. It affects our bodies' chemistry and makes us wants those foods. If you think of chocolate, chocolate is a really good mixture of sugar and fat, and we know that chocolate is so pleasurable. And so it makes us want to eat it.

Q: How do you deal with cravings for junk when you're trying to change your diet?
Thomas: It comes down to moderation, and it comes down to choice and taking responsibility. Of course you can eat chocolate. You just don't want to replace fruits and vegetables with chocolate. You just have to learn what the right foods are and make some good choices and balance it out.

About those cravings, don't deprive yourself of food. There are so many diets out there and sometimes we are afraid of food. And so we say, "I'm never going to have cake," or "I'm never going to have ice cream." And then what happens is that's not realistic and we want them so bad and then we end up eating too much of them.

So allow yourself to have the foods you enjoy but make responsible decisions so the majority of the foods you're eating are healthy and nutritious. And that [only] every now and then you're having something that's high in sugar or fat.

Q: How important is it for us to read food labels and what do they tell you?
Thomas: Labels are a really helpful tool for making good food decisions. Always look at the serving size, because everything there is related to one serving. You might look at a bag of chips and say, "Oh, it's only 150 calories," but the serving size is five chips.

With super-sizing, Snickers are so huge now, and bags of chips in vending machines are not one serving now, they're two. And so we're getting bigger and bigger.

> You don't have to eat carrots and celery every day.

So it comes back to choice and responsibility. And part of that responsibility is knowing how to be an informed consumer. The other thing to do is look at the ingredients listed there. The ingredients are listed in the order of the amount that's in there. So if you see sugar as the first ingredient, you know that a lot of the carbohydrates listed are in there as simple sugars.

Q: What are carbohydrates? Are there good carbs and bad carbs?
Thomas: Carbohydrates are an energy source. They give us the energy we need to go about the day. They're found in a whole variety of different foods: whole grains, cereals, pasta, rice, potatoes.

There's different types of carbohydrates, and that's where learning about nutrition comes in. There's what we call complex carbohydrates—they're the breads, pastas, rice, potatoes. In terms of nutrition it's better to pick whole grains—whole wheat bread, brown rice. And then there's the refined carbohydrates, the simple sugars: honey, table sugar, sweets, candy. We want our diet to be more of the whole grain carbohydrates than the simple sugars.

Q: What do you have to say to teens who want to try the low-carb diets that are so popular these days?
Thomas: The low-carb diets that eliminate all carbohydrates deprive our bodies of nutritious foods. Fruit has sugar in it, milk has sugar in it, and low-carb diets tend to cut these things out or way down. But we need the nutrients in those foods to help prevent disease down the road, like heart disease, diabetes, some cancers.

> A healthy diet and exercising are the keys to staying healthy.

Low-carb dieters lose the weight fast, but they tend to gain it back when they stop dieting. What I'd tell teenagers who are interested in losing weight is that fad diets are not the way to go. It's better to eat smaller portions of a variety of balanced foods, and to be more physically active. Eating a healthy diet and exercising are still the keys to maintaining a good weight and staying healthy.

Q: Are meal-replacement drinks helpful for teens trying to eat healthy quickly?
Thomas: An important nutrient that's often not found in those foods is fiber. If you think about an apple versus apple juice, there's a lot of fiber in the apple skin and that's really good for you in terms of your overall health and disease prevention. If you drink apple juice you're not getting any of that fiber. But you're getting a lot of calories because you have to squeeze a lot of apples to get one glass of apple juice.

One of the most important things you can do is get a wide variety of foods—different types of fruits, vegetables, grains, meats or proteins—because all foods have different kinds of nutrients.

MY HOOD IS BAD FOR MY HEALTH

By Anonymous

Every afternoon my abuela (grandmother) walks down the squeaky steps leading to our kitchen. When she hops into that apron, I know it's my cue to run for cover.

Making up her own recipes is how my abuela relieves her stress. She puts all her worries behind her when she takes on her mission: What's for dinner?

With a dash of this and a sprinkle of that her creations are ready. I admit that my abuela performs miracles. She stretches her budget by mixing leftovers with fresh foods, is obsessed with cooking pork in every meal, adds plenty of grease and oil—and people savor every last taste. I think it's disgusting.

My abuela is always talking about how to save a dollar. She's collected a huge stack of rusty, beat-up cans of food from the church pantry. She also frequents the tons of 99¢ stores that have opened in my neighborhood. My grandmother brings home 99¢ juice, sodas, and junk foods that taste like complete crap and have no nutritional value.

I get angry and frustrated with this woman. Why is she so hardheaded? She talks about saving a dollar, but if we have enough money for Direct TV and all the HBO channels she orders, I think we can afford some healthier, fresher food, instead of eating like it's hard times.

But if I complain to my abuela, she looks at me with disappointment and says, "Well, you don't know what it is to not have. It's called survival."

Like many people in my neighborhood, my abuela comes from a really poor background. Putting food on the table was an everyday struggle in her family. Every bit of food was considered a blessing.

Moving to the U.S. from Panama has been a big transition for her. Every day she sees food going to waste, while people in poor countries are starving. I understand my grandmother's attitude, but at times she acts as if we're standing directly on the poverty line, when I know that we could spend our money on food if we saved it somewhere else.

I think what we put in our bodies should be one of my family's biggest concerns. I began feeling conscious of how I eat last spring, when I started noticing how depressed and moody I was. A friend told me that "You are what you eat" is not just a saying. What you eat really can affect your performance in everyday life. If you're eating a lot of sugary foods, your mood can swing wildly, or if you're eating too much you can feel drowsy and bored.

At that time, my face was breaking out and my stomach was never agreeing with me. I would wake up nauseous, and get severe headaches that left me looking like an insane witch by the end of the day. I know what's healthy and what isn't, but I was constantly eating junk at fast food restaurants or running to the corner store for a pint of Haagen Dazs every time I felt depressed. Over the summer, I joined a nutrition workshop. When I began reading the nutritional facts on the back of cartons, I started thinking about the vitamins, fat, and protein that each food has to offer. I stopped going to the corner store for candy every time I had spare change.

Then we got to buy a week's worth of healthy food. I took my healthy week seriously. I drank tons more water and ate more veggies. I started using substitutes for sugar, like honey and fruits. Whenever I had an urgent craving for a sweet, crispy, layered cheese Danish, I settled for a granola bar or a tall glass of vanilla soy milk.

My first time drinking soy milk was not easy. When I tasted it, I immediately spat it out. But because I felt it was a step toward improving my health, I began to drink a glass each day. My taste buds adapted. The more I drank it, the better it began to taste.

Now I'm a soy fan. Every time my abuela goes to the supermarket, I beg her to buy me soy milk. Sometimes she'll refuse and say it's too expensive. So I put aside money to buy my soy milk every week.

Though healthy eating took an adjustment, I was feeling great! No more of that oily feeling I would get when I ate greasy foods. After an icy glass of soy milk, I felt like I could take on the world.

I also began taking nature walks around a big park, enjoying Earth's green kingdom. It felt good to take care of myself. I loved thinking about healthy foods nourishing every inch of me. I felt like I was doing myself a favor, so I vowed to continue to eat healthier.

But eating healthy in my neighborhood—Brownsville, Brooklyn—is a challenge. My neighborhood is grim, with worn-down and torn looking houses and projects surrounded by nothing but fast-food restaurants, Chinese take-outs, and fried chicken spots filled with miserable obese people.

Sure the food is cheap. There's a bargain everywhere you go. But you're only getting what you pay for—unhealthy processed and fried food. The Kennedy Fried Chicken place even gives out free sodas with every meal. Why can't they give out bottled water or juice for a change?

I know why people eat in those places. If you're looking for a meal that fills you up for cheap, you can go to Wendy's and buy up the dollar menu—the more the merrier—or eat at the Chinese restaurants. You can buy only junk if you're hungry without much in your wallet.

As much as I want to stay healthy, I hate having to stretch $5 to buy a meal. Sometimes I buy an Ensure and a banana nut muffin, or a veggie slice from the pizza store, and find myself hungry in an hour.

> I long for the fresh taste of organic fruit.

I'm proud of myself for trying to eat healthy despite my budget. But my abuela has been quite upset with my new diet. She feels my new way of eating healthy is a cry of hunger, because I've lost a little weight. She looks at me and says, "Why is your face so pale? You look so skinny! The only piece of fat you got there is that little bump called a behind."

Not so thrilled with the comment, I leave the room as she laughs up a storm. My grandma defines healthy people as those with meat, and glowing skin and hair. In her eyes, I'm bony and making a fool out of myself by not eating the food she serves. Food is food. There is no such thing as bad or good. You eat when you have and starve when you don't.

For now, my abuela laughs and figures I'll learn. But I long for the fresh taste of organic fruit on my tongue. Opening my refrigerator brings me back to the cold taste of reality: Bread full of mold, a pack of nearly rotten sausages, microwave dinners, and of bunch of God knows what decaying in a plastic container for who knows how long.

Eyes see, brain picks up data, stomach growls in response. With that I go to bed, another night of an unsatisfied stomach. I lie in bed wishing it would all go away: Poverty, my neighborhood, my grandmother's cooking, my headache.

Maybe I'm ungrateful or stubborn. (Why can't I just give in and eat unhealthy food like everyone else does? Hey, at least there's more on your plate.) But my anger bursts like a cannon scattering balls of depression. Why is my neighborhood such a threat to our health? Why are healthy foods out of reach of the poor? We all know people who are suffering because of their eating habits—they're dealing with diabetes, high cholesterol, or hypertension.

As darkness falls, my stomach's growling leads my mind through twists and turns. "You're hungry," I tell myself. "Get something to eat. That's better than no food at all."

> **Why are healthy foods out of reach of the poor?**

Finally I scurry down to our kitchen, ignoring the tall tower of dishes in the sink and the mountains of crumbs and the stains splattered about the kitchen counter. Opening the refrigerator door, a silhouette gleaming in the light catches my eye. It's a box of soy milk. Abuela must have bought it for me!

I pick it up with relief and remember the discussion I had with my abuela days ago about my newfound love of soy. Usually our discussions end with "I'm the adult and you're the child," but to my surprise, she listened for a change.

The writer was in high school when she wrote this story.
She later graduated and enrolled in college.

MALE ON THE SCALE

By Anonymous

I am a male anorexic. I finally admitted it. If you saw me, you probably wouldn't know. Actually, nobody really suspects it. When I hang out with people and they want something to eat, I just say I'm not that hungry and nibble on some fries.

On average, I eat one meal a day, and maybe a peanut butter and jelly sandwich an hour later. I skip breakfast and I skip lunch. I eat dinner because I have to, though if I can get away with it, I won't. I don't fully understand why I do it. I just do.

Let me stop lying—I know exactly why. It started when I came out of rehab. I was fat because the only thing you do is eat and sleep and sit all day. When I got out I was 187 pounds, about 50 pounds heavier than I'd been only three months before.

I didn't really worry about it until my friends started to tease me. Everybody was like, "Damn, you fat now." People who I used to tease finally had something to get back at me about. A kid who was always chubby would come up to me like, "Damn, what happened to you? You used to be all built and skinny. Now look at your fat butt!" I had to deal with this every day.

To me, being fat was like having a scarlet letter on my chest. I mean, fat people are the ones who get picked on the most. When I was skinny, everybody didn't have jokes, but when I was fat, I got cracked on everywhere.

I started to beat myself up mentally. I'd go shopping for pants and be mad that I couldn't fit in a 34 and still have them baggy. I was mad 'cause my fingers had gotten so fat my ring wouldn't fit. I was a pretty boy before I got fat, but after, I was too afraid to walk around in "wife beaters" and open shirts, 'cause the fat jokes would never end.

> Fat people are the ones who get picked on the most.

I was so ashamed, I let it get to me. I'd look at myself in the mirror and curse at my body. I'd tell myself I was the ugliest and fattest person I'd ever seen. I became hateful of my new weight and decided it had to go.

At first I was eating like I have my whole life: at least two servings of every meal, one if it was nasty. But one night I decided to see if I could make myself throw up after I ate dinner. A friend of mine had confided to me that before I met her she was fat, but she started to throw up her food and that's how she was able to look the way she did.

I thought about what she said and decided to try it myself. It was hard the first time. I thought I was gonna throw up my stomach! But about a week or two after that, I would throw up dinner four times out of the week. Then I started to do the same thing after lunch.

One time, I got caught in the act. I was in the bathroom, head over the toilet, when my roommate rushed in to get me. He was like, "What you been doing?"

I said, "I just feel sick." Luckily, it didn't go further than that. After a while, though, I started to make myself hate food.

I stopped eating breakfast and lunch altogether. It was hard; I was hungry all the time. But I became accustomed to it.

I'm not fat anymore, but I fear ever being fat again. A few friends know about this, and they worry about me. They think it may have consequences, but so far I haven't seen any.

Still, since I started to write this story, I've begun to realize that I need to stop not eating. I've been getting a little better. I eat more—two meals instead of one.

The author was in high school when he wrote this story.

SCALING BACK

By Erica Harrigan

When I was 12, eating became a way to soothe myself. That year I was admitted into a mental institution to deal with the anger I had from being abused as a child.

At the mental hospital, I started taking anti-depressants. The medicine helped my moods but made me into a pig—and I was already a big eater. I would eat five times a day: Breakfast, lunch, dinner and two snacks, and I always had seconds at breakfast and thirds at lunch and dinner. (If they hadn't given me a limit, I probably would've had seconds of snacks, too.)

I would eat, then go straight to my room and sleep all day. I slept so much because I felt depressed. Even though I felt safe in the hospital, I wanted to be free. I felt like I was locked up in a cage.

I also isolated myself because if I interacted with the other kids, they would drive me to the point of flipping out and I would misbehave. If one person acted out we all got penalized for it.

If I was doing well and one person acted stupid and ruined everything, I'd just explode and attack whoever stepped out of line. Other times, I was the one who acted up. Then I'd get restrained and medicated.

After two or three months in the hospital, I went from about 70 pounds to 300 pounds. I just blew up. I actually felt good about gaining weight. When I was skinny, people made fun of me, calling me "sacks of bones" and "crack baby." Those names hurt.

I also liked being overweight because I'd been raped when I was 9, and I used to think I was raped because I was sexy. (Later I realized I was just a kid, and that my looks had nothing to do with it.) I believed that being fat would make me unattractive to guys, so I felt safe.

But when I was older, I got moved to a residential treatment center, went off the medication that had made me gain a lot of weight, and dropped 150 pounds.

I'd eat like a pig when I was angry.

On weekends I stayed with family in Harlem and hung out with my cousin. My cousin was like a sister or a role model to me. Anything she did I wanted to do. I got my tongue pierced and a nose ring because she did. We went out together to clubs and parties.

My cousin liked to play boys so I tried to do the same. The more I visited my aunt's crib, the more I became hot in the pants. One day, on a dare, I had sex. I didn't like it, but I liked the feeling of being accepted by the boys in my hood. After that I had sex just to be down, and instead of using food to calm myself, I used sex to make myself feel wanted and accepted.

I really didn't enjoy the sex with any guys, because it made me remember my past experiences. But I wanted love, and I thought that was how I could get it. It took a long time for me to come to my senses and realize that, once again, I was hurting myself by letting my body get out of my control.

Truthfully, I needed help to take more control of my body. I couldn't imagine how I could calm myself down without being addicted to food or sex.

My current boyfriend showed me what true love is all about. He told me, "Love isn't just about sex. Sex is only part of the relationship. A relationship is about support, communication, affection, and loyalty."

I started to realize that a guy could like me for myself, not for my body. With his help, I stopped sleeping around. It was hard because sex was a comfort to me, even though it was also scary and depressing.

After I calmed down on sex, I noticed that when I was feeling emotional, I'd eat. I'd eat like a pig when I was angry and like a garbage truck when I was sad. When I was lonely,

> I felt scared putting my health at risk.

I'd eat 'til my belly was stuffed. After I stuffed myself, I'd feel greedy, like I was a fat slob taking in all the food I could eat. It was almost the same emotions for me as having sex: I'd feel good while I was eating, but afterward I'd feel nasty.

One time my boyfriend left New York for a weekend. I felt lonely. I called him constantly and got no answer. I was worried so I isolated myself and ate half of what was in the refrigerator: hot dogs, sandwiches, cereal. I would have helped myself to the rest but, luckily, I had to think about my roommates. I didn't want them to starve.

A few months ago, though, I decided that if I could take control of my sexuality, I could take control of my eating. I felt scared that I was putting my health at risk. I knew I ate too much fat and junk food and drank a lot of sugary sodas. I wanted to begin taking care of myself better, so I decided to eat healthier foods.

I began to cut down on pork and beef, because they're fattening and can give you high cholesterol. I came up with substitutes like turkey and tuna fish, which are lower in fat.

I ate more vegetables, such as spinach, peas, carrots, and corn. (For a while I went overboard on the corn, eating five to ten cans a week. Then I found out corn has a lot of sugar, so I started to cut back.) I also ate more plums and grapes, apples and oranges, and my favorite fruit, mangos.

At first it was hard to balance my meals. I craved junk food, and felt hungry a lot. But eventually, eating healthy became a habit. I felt proud that I tried to change a way of living that was hurting me and succeeded. Taking control of my sex life and my eating habits makes me feel I'm capable of doing anything.

Since I've been eating healthier, I've had more energy. I've also noticed that I have dropped a few pounds. I didn't mean to be dieting. I felt fine about how I looked and just wanted to be healthier. But I'm glad to know that changing what I eat is having an impact on my body.

The biggest change is that I rarely eat just to eat now. I try to eat only when I'm hungry. I feel healthier and stronger, and my will power is stronger. Most important, I feel my body is much more under my own control.

Erica was 19 when she wrote this story.
She later married and had two children.

THE WOULD-BE VEGETARIAN

By Suzy Berkowitz

"More spam," I thought, opening the forwarded e-mail that cluttered my inbox. A small paragraph encouraging vegetarianism was followed by a link to a video on the website of the organization PETA (People for the Ethical Treatment of Animals). I squinted curiously and opened the link.

For the next ten minutes I sat, eyes glued to the screen, watching a gruesome documentary on slaughterhouses. The video contained clips of baby pigs being shot, live bulls being castrated, and other horrifying images. Some of it made me cry, some of it made me gasp, but all of it made me disgusted. I had never before thought about becoming a vegetarian, but after watching that video, I felt it would be an insult to every animal in the world to continue eating meat. I felt personally responsible for their lives. "We are their voice," I told myself. "If we don't do something, who will?"

But becoming a vegetarian, regardless of how much I wanted to stop eating meat, was all but impossible for me. I grew up in a house full of carnivores. My entire family cooked and ate steak constantly, and my mother looked down on vegetarians, especially teenage ones. "You're a growing girl, you need meat," she'd respond when I began to talk about vegetarianism.

Though I never dared hint to her that I was interested in becoming a vegetarian myself, she often drew that conclusion, leaping down my throat with a vengeance: "Don't even try to stop eating meat," she'd yell. "It's good for your blood!"

To I spent two weeks as a closet vegetarian: not eating meat, and doing everything in my power to keep my mom from finding out about it. I spent as little time as possible at home. I'd eat salads for lunch, and cook myself spaghetti before my mom came home from work.

I distinctly remember having to turn down turkey bacon one Saturday morning when my mom made that, along with an omelet, for breakfast. The smell of the bacon crept up my nose, tempting me like some kind of sinful force.

"No," I thought, staring at the meat on my plate. "I'm a vegetarian." It felt good to say it in my head, like I stood for something. I pretended I wasn't hungry. My mom just rolled her eyes.

I apologized to the chicken.

Then, one night, I went to a diner with my mom and one of her friends. I was having trouble deciding what to eat, as usual, so my mom took charge and ordered me chicken noodle soup. My heart raced. "How am I going to do this?" I thought. I looked at the people sitting near me, casually munching meatloaf or sucking on a chicken bone. "Those animals were tortured, you know," I felt like screaming.

The waiter sprinted back to our table, placing the cup of soup in front of me. Inside floated noodles and strips of gray meat. I stared down at it and imagined the chicken being alive. I could feel my mom's eyes on me. I didn't want to have it out with her, not there, not then, so I sighed, picked up my spoon, and inwardly apologized to the chicken.

That night at the diner was a reality check. My mom's opinions on the benefits of meat were too solid to be challenged, and living under her roof meant her word was set in stone. Becoming a complete vegetarian wasn't a viable option for me.

Regardless, I still wanted to do something for animals, something that would feel significant. Then I thought about fast food. I had seen the documentary *Super-Size Me* a few years back, in Hebrew school, and was therefore aware of how unhealthy fast food was. (The documentary follows the filmmaker as he eats nothing but McDonald's food for one month, and shows how his health suffers because of his diet.)

Being 13 at the time, and not fully understanding the health risks or animal cruelty that go along with meaty fast-food meals, I'd continued ordering burgers and nuggets without a thought. But after my failed attempt at becoming a complete vegetarian, I remembered the documentary and realized that giving up fast-food meat was not only good for the animals, but for me as well. I decided that doing without fast-food meat would be my contribution.

I didn't tell my mom about this decision at first, because I knew she would scorn even a restriction that minuscule, but eventually she found out. She reacted with an eye roll, convincing herself it was just a phase I was going through, and continued muttering about vegetarianism being the newest fad among teens.

My friends still laugh when I order a salad.

Initially, I didn't think abstaining from fast food meat was much of a contribution. But after a few weeks, it was all I wanted. Standing in line at a McDonald's one lunchtime, I had my eye on the crispy chicken snack wrap. Just one wouldn't hurt—the chicken was already dead, anyway. My stomach debated against my head for a good five minutes, the thought of sweet honey mustard and crunchy chicken wrapped in that savory flour tortilla sending chills down my spine.

When I stepped up to the counter, though, I took a deep breath and ordered fries. Craving chicken but ordering something no animals had been killed to produce was a big sacrifice, I realized. I was proud of my will power.

And since then—for the past year and a half—I haven't taken a bite of fast-food meat. When I start college this fall, I plan to become a pescatarian, basically a vegetarian who eats fish. It'll be much easier to control my own diet because I'll be living away from home, away from everyone who disapproves of me not eating meat.

I try to avoid talking about these plans as much as I can when I'm around my mom, because I know she strongly disagrees with them. She knows there's little she can do about it once I've moved out of the house, and realizing my mind has been made up, she doesn't bring it up either.

But until college, I'm sticking to my current contribution, and learning to tolerate its challenges. I occasionally crave a McDonald's snack wrap during those lunch breaks from my job when I'm overwhelmed with hunger. I have to remind myself that by not eating meat, I am saving the life of an animal somewhere.

My mom still orders me hamburgers when we go to fast-food restaurants, shaking her head when I refuse to eat them, and many of my friends still laugh when I order a salad instead of a sandwich. Some of my family members simply don't understand my sacrifice, and many of them try to convince me that meat is an essential part of our natural food chain.

I nod along when they argue, but I never take their arguments into consideration. For every person in my life who disapproves of my refusal to eat fast food meat, there is one person who thinks of it as an admirable sacrifice. I may only be one person, and for now, I do still eat meat at home. But I consider my contribution something to be proud of, simply because it's mine. And I'm happy that, regardless of the obstacles, for now I've found a compromise between what I am allowed to do and what I know I should do.

Suzy was 17 when she wrote this story.
She went to Adelphi University.

CARNIVORE NO MORE

By Kamaal Dashiem Crumpton

"Here Kamaal, take this," said my foster mom Crystal. She
handed me a plate of rice, corn, and baked chicken.

"Umm . . . would you mind if I had soup instead?" I knew
if I tried to explain my new decision that she would give me
her long-winded opinion. I wasn't trying to hide it from her,
just to avoid that conversation for a while longer.

"No, Kamaal. You have dinner ready right in front of you.
Why would you rather eat soup?"

There was a brief pause and then I had to tell her: "I'm not
eating meat anymore."

"All meat? That's really cutting away from the nutrients
that you need."

Changing your diet is hard in foster care. Crystal and her
husband Jaime Sr. have four other foster children besides me:
Uzzia, Arinze, Jose, and Devante. Their biological sons are
Xavier and Jaime Jr.

There are many different eating habits in the house.
Jaime Sr. is religious and fasts on occasion. Xavier does not
eat beef because he says it blows him up. Arinze and Jose eat
everything except for fish, which boggles my mind because

seafood tastes so good to me. Uzzia, Devante, and Jamie Jr. pretty much eat everything in the book.

Most of the time we don't all eat together; Crystal usually eats upstairs by herself. Some days Crystal makes dinner for us; other days she has a friend from church come over with Chinese food or spare ribs or a chicken salad. I knew she wasn't going to start making tofu dishes just for me!

A Friend's Example

I decided to become a vegetarian six months ago. My friend Imani told me she was a vegetarian. Being around her pushed me to eat healthier. Before I would rather buy a bag of chips than a banana. But when we ate together, I would eat more like her, and mostly everything Imani eats is healthy. (I didn't know what Naked Juice was before I met her.)

I started to eat something green (my favorite color) every day. I looked up soy products, different cheeses, different oils, and other foods I had never heard of before on Google Scholar.

I decided to keep eating fish and other seafood because it was healthier than beef, chicken, and pork products. I learned that the word for vegetarians who eat fish (like me and Imani) is "pescatarians."

Downsides to Meat

For most of my life, I've loved eating meat—chicken, beef, lamb, and turkey, everything except pork. Because of my father's religious beliefs, he raised me and the rest of the family not eating pork. He told us the pig was a dirty animal that plays, bathes in, and even eats its own filth. That was enough reason for me not to eat it.

But then I began to wonder if pigs were the only animals that were disgusting in their habits or were raised in an unhealthy way. Imani told me that she actually eats meat in Jamaica because the animals raised there are much healthier than those raised in America.

So I did some research. I found several bad practices that farmers use to raise their animals that are cruel to us and them alike. Most cattle in the U.S. in big "factory farms" are raised eating corn instead of grass because it is cheaper. But corn is not an appropriate diet for cows, and corn-fed cows' meat is more likely to have harmful E. coli bacteria in it, according to a book called Fat, Inc.

Factory-farmed animals are crowded together in unsanitary conditions, so farmers give them low levels of antibiotics to prevent disease. This creates bacteria resistant to antibiotics—a huge public health problem. To make cows grow and produce milk faster, factory farms inject them with hormones, which harms the health of people who consume their beef or milk.

Substitutes
I wasn't sure about which nutrients I would miss by giving up meat. I found out that B-12, a vitamin usually found in meat, makes blood cells strong and keeps nerves intact for proper brain function. So I take a multi-vitamin with B-12.

Teenage boys need protein, which builds muscle mass. Luckily fish and any other seafood are packed with it. Shrimp, crab, lobster, and tuna all are full of protein and not that much fat. Because I also eat soy products, eggs, cheese, and nuts, I don't have to worry about not getting my share.

After I dropped meat, I wanted to cut out everything unhealthy that I could, from soda to chips. I learned that high fructose corn syrup (HFCS) is in almost everything that we eat because it is cheap and makes food taste more appealing. Yet eating this contributes to obesity and type 2 diabetes, which have been leading causes of death in the U.S. for over three decades.

I can't imagine sitting down morning, noon, and night eating corn for the rest of my life, yet it's happening to people and they do not know it. It's in cereal and other snacks, as well as in that corn-fed beef.

My main motivation for giving up meat was the greater good of my body. But it's turned out to be a cool way to save money, too. Going to the closest McDonald's or chicken spot around the corner cost me a lot more than spaghetti or rice and peas that I would be able to whip up at my house. I'm tempted by all the vegetarian dishes and restaurants in New York, but mostly I eat at home.

I can't say that meat doesn't smell good to me, even pork. There have been times when my foster mother makes certain meat dishes, and the look and smell consume my insides.

But I have learned not to rely only on my impulses. I stick with the belief that changing the way I eat is going to help me. Eating organic foods (foods made without pesticides or other chemicals) as much as I can, ridding my body of excess sugar, and lowering my cholesterol are some things I have grown very fond of. I haven't seen any big change (I was already thin and healthy), but I like knowing that I'm eating healthier.

Obstacles

What has been a bigger problem than meat cravings are other people. The other day I was given chicken by a friend, and it devastated her when I told her that I wouldn't eat it.

"Eat it Kamaal, you're a carnivore! It'll be just like old times," my friend demanded.

"If anything, I was an omnivore. And me eating meat doesn't have anything to do with the good old days," I replied, laughing.

"Eat it," she fired back at me with a menacing glare in her eyes. People can be so wrapped up in their own beliefs and customs!

I have yet to ask my foster mom to make a special veggie dish or fish for dinner. But she may be softening up about my choices. Last night my dinner was very satisfying (even though it was all carbs); a lot of rice, string beans, and macaroni and cheese. I had two plates and fell asleep like a baby.

I'm enjoying life as a vegetarian. There are many substitutes for meat that are healthier for you, such as falafel and tofu. It seems to me that many people eat meat only because that's what they're used to. But in the end, isn't a little change worth a healthier, longer life?

A TALE OF TWO FOOD CHAINS

YC Staff

Processed Food

To prepare them for a long shelf life in the supermarket, highly processed foods are altered radically from their natural state. Often, nutrients are removed and chemicals are added. Nutritionists trace the rise of obesity and diet-related illnesses to the large-scale consumption of highly processed food. Not sure if something is a highly processed food? Three clues: it comes in a package, the ingredient list has lots of stuff you can't pronounce, and the expiration date is months away.

Subsidies
Since 1973, the U.S. government has paid farmers subsidies to grow corn and soy, making it profitable to produce these crops in large quantities. Because of subsidies, corn and soy have become staples of the American diet—check the label nearest you for corn and soy products!

When subsidies made corn cheap, scientists invented highfructose corn syrup, a sweetener that has a longer shelf life and is easier to transport than sugar. Critics say that this artificial sweetener, which is produced in a laboratory, is metabolized by your body differently than sugar and contributes to the obesity epidemic.

During processing, high-fructose corn syrup and other additives may be added to food products. These additives—like preservatives, food dyes, and artificial flavors—are included to enhance a product's flavor and appearance. (Some additives are actually designed to stimulate appetite, which triggers overeating.) Along with additives, many processed foods contain partially hydrogenated oils, which are liquid vegetable oils that have had hydrogen added to them. These oils produce artificial trans fats, which have been found to raise cholesterol and increase the risk of heart disease and stroke. (Thankfully, it's easier than ever to limit the amount of trans fat in your diet: The government now requires that nutrition labels include trans fat information. Plus, in 2005, New York City schools got rid of trans fats and, a year later, they were banned from all city restaurants.)

Factory Farms

Factory farms raise and slaughter livestock (cattle, pigs, chicken, and turkeys) in cramped spaces, which can become a breeding ground for bacteria like E. coli, which can kill you. Animals are fed corn, which isn't part of their natural diet and can make them sick. To prevent the animals from getting sick, they are regularly fed antibiotics that we, in turn, consume by eating the animals. Most of the meat in the U.S. comes from factory farms.

Whole Foods

Foods that are exactly as grown in nature are called whole foods (apples would be one example). When you alter the food a little by adding a few ingredients or preservatives, then it becomes a minimally processed food (like apple sauce). If it's altered a lot (like an apple-flavored Pop Tart), it becomes a

> Whole foods are considered the most nutritious.

highly processed food. Whole foods are generally considered the most nutritious.

Grass Fed

Cows are healthiest and leanest when they eat their natural diet of grass. Many people believe grass-fed beef tastes better than cornor grain-fed beef, although it's more costly and timeconsuming to raise cattle on grass.

Free Range Chicken and Eggs

According to the USDA, chicken and eggs that are labeled "free range" or "free roaming" come from chickens that are allowed outdoors.

Organic Farming

Organic farming is a method of growing crops without using chemical pesticides, weed killers, or fertilizers, and raising livestock without antibiotics or growth hormones. Organic farming tends be more environmentally friendly, and advocates say food produced organically is healthier than non-organic food. However, it's harder to grow food organically, making it more expensive than non-organic food.

Farmers' market

A farmers' market is a place where small-scale farmers and other producers of whole or minimally processed foods (like fresh bread, cheese, or organic milk) gather to sell their goods directly to consumers. Farmers' markets are great places to find fresh, organic, and nutritious local food. Local food is more environmentally friendly than food shipped from thousands of miles away. Plus, it usually tastes better.

More Tips for Healthy Eating
YC Staff

Wait Out the Cravings
Whenever you're craving that sugary snack, stop and wait 15 minutes. Cravings will often pass with time.

Combine When You Dine
The combination of protein, fiber, and a little fat will satisfy your belly the best. For a filling snack, try a piece of whole wheat toast (fiber) with a smear of peanut butter (fat and protein), or a piece of cheese (fat and protein) with an apple (fiber).

Skipping Meals Is Not Ideal
It's important to eat something healthy in the morning, even if you're not very hungry. This way you have the strength to make it through the day without resorting to vending machines or fast food.

If You're Able, Read the Label
Know what's in your food. If the list of ingredients is long and contains lots of things you can't pronounce, look for something else.

Soda Is a No, Duh
Soda is liquid sugar. Many health experts say an increase in soda consumption is a big contributor to the obesity epidemic. Trade in soda for seltzer or water.

Can the Confusion
Confused by conflicting health advice? Stick to this mantra from author Michael Pollan: "Eat food. Not too much. Mostly plants." ("Food" meaning whole foods instead of highly processed "foodlike substances.")

Eat to Get Full, Not to Be Wasteful
Don't serve yourself more food than you actually need just because it's tasty. It takes a while for your stomach to register fullness, so eat slowly. Have a second helping only if you still feel hungry after about twenty minutes.

Reduce the Juice
You should get your calories from food, not juice, so trade in high-calorie orange juice for a filling, fiber-rich, low-calorie orange.

If you want to know more about . . .
A balanced diet and making healthy food choices: www.hsph. harvard.edu/nutritionsource/

The environmental and health impact of products you buy, from food to shampoo: www.goodguide.com

Where to find farms, farmer's markets, or food and nutrition programs in your neighborhood: www.eatwellguide.org

Cooking with teen-friendly recipes: www.kidshealth.org/teen/recipes

PART THREE

STAYING HEALTHY:
DEALING WITH STRESS

I Won't Let Asthma Rule My Life

By Viveca Shearin

From the moment I was born, I had trouble breathing on my own. The doctors told my parents I had asthma, a respiratory disease that affects the airways (the tubes carrying air in and out of your lungs) and can be life-threatening.

When I was little, I got an asthma attack at least twice a month and went to the hospital a lot. When I got an attack, the pain was like a dagger being plunged into my chest and twisted over and over, and it was hard to breathe. The pain only went away if I stayed still.

Having an attack was scary, but I always forgot about it afterward. I was still young, so I didn't have a grip on my situation yet. I did what other little kids did—I had fun and I acted as if I didn't have a care in the world. When I think back to my years of fun and youth, I'm glad I enjoyed them, because I was about to face reality.

One evening when I was 10, I was watching TV with my sisters in the living room when, without warning, I felt a sharp pain in my chest. I tried the inhaler my parents had just gotten for me, but it didn't work. I told my mom and she asked me, "Do you want to go to the hospital?" I didn't want her to take me because I knew we'd be there all night. I hated my asthma because at times like this, I felt like a burden to my parents, making them go out of their way for me.

But the pain in my chest was getting worse, so we got dressed and told my sisters that we'd be back late. In the emergency room, we went to sign in and I was horrified at all of the names that were already on the list. I knew this was going to be a long night.

We found seats among the many occupied ones. I wanted nothing more than to just lie on the floor and sleep amongst the sounds of phones ringing, babies crying and people talking. The pains in my chest kept going on and off as I tried to find a comfortable position in my chair. It was two or three hours before my name was called.

When I finally got to the examination room, the doctor put the cold metal of her stethoscope on my chest. "Breathe in and out," she said. Then she hooked me up to a machine that was like a giant inhaler. It had some liquid in a little case that turned into vapor. "Keep inhaling until the liquid is all gone," she said.

My mother sat down beside me, grabbed my hand and gave me her usual smile that told me that everything was going to be all right. As I inhaled the vapor, I began to feel relieved. The pain in my chest was going down. But I was also angry at the long wait, and very tired. It was after 2 a.m. when we left the hospital.

After that, I swore that I would take better care of my asthma so that my mother and I wouldn't have to spend another night at the hospital. I knew from my parents and doctors that asthma attacks can be triggered by things like dust, pollutants, smoke, and pesticides. So to prevent another attack, I started making an extreme effort to avoid anything that could be a trigger.

One day as I was walking to the store, I stopped short of several adults who were smoking cigarettes and cigars in the middle of the sidewalk. I told myself that it was just smoke, but in the back of my mind, I was saying, "It isn't just smoke. It could really harm me if I inhale it." Nervousness and bravery argued back and forth inside of me, but my nervousness finally won out. I crossed the street to avoid the smokers and continued on my way to the store.

Soon my life became ruled by my fear of an asthma attack. I became paranoid, worrying that whatever I did could trigger an attack. If I was eating something and my chest started hurting, I stopped eating it immediately because I thought it might contain ingredients that could mess with my asthma.

If I was out with my family and we passed somebody smoking, I'd hold my breath and wait for the nauseating, toxic smell to pass before I'd let go of my breath. I always made sure no one was looking when I did it, because I didn't want my family to suspect anything was wrong.

I began staying in the house more, only leaving to go to school or to the store. When kids in the neighborhood asked me why I stayed inside all the time, I said that I was scared of the sound of gunshots in our neighborhood. That was partly true, but I didn't tell them that what I was more scared of was getting an asthma attack.

I promised to not get so stressed over my asthma.

I stayed in that house for months, angry and sad, watching the other kids playing and wishing for a day when I could take off my asthmatic shell and join them. But the world isn't fair. It doesn't change its direction for one person.

My antics kept me out of the doors of that godforsaken hospital. My asthma was better, but now I was trapped by my obsession with avoiding an attack. I was making things better, but worse at the same time.

Not only did it start to interrupt my daily routines like school and chores, but my family had started to notice as well. They asked me why I didn't play outside anymore. To spare myself the embarrassment, I told them I was afraid of all the gang activity in our neighborhood.

By the time I was in junior high school, I was exhausted. I was sick of feeling scared of my asthma. On New Year's Eve, when I was 11 years old, I decided to take my life back.

My family and I were in the living room waiting for the ball to drop on TV. As we were feasting on chips and dip, deviled eggs and champagne, I thought to myself, "Maybe it's time to make a change." It felt appropriate since New Year's is a time for making changes.

I made a resolution for myself in my head. I promised to take it easier and to not get so stressed over my asthma. Then the ball began the final countdown. "Five, four, three, two, one! Happy New Year!" we shouted, clinking our champagne glasses. It felt like my family and all of America was joining in to welcome not only a new year, but a new me.

I put my new resolution to the test right away. At first, it was a little scary being outside and open to most asthma triggers. I had to mentally coach myself, saying, "You can't be like this for the rest of your life. You have to take a risk sometime, and that time is now."

For starters, I stopped making a detour anytime I saw someone smoking a cigarette. I told myself, "If I don't breathe in the smoke, I'll be all right." I still kept my mouth shut while walking through the smoke and was careful not to breathe it in, but I tried not to be as paranoid about it as before.

Then I tried to get back into the spirit of playing outside again. I ran and played even though my chest was hurting, and I reassured myself that it was all right. Nothing bad happened. After a while, I started to feel more relaxed.

One day that summer, I went outside with a book and sat on the stoop to read. It was a little hot out, so I sat in the shade. The wind was blowing gently and it was quiet. Then my next-door neighbor and his friends came outside to smoke.

> I have control of my asthma and not the other way around.

Normally, I would have gone back in the house to read. This time, I took my book and sat down on the bench opposite the stoop. The nearby smoke didn't stop me from enjoying my afternoon. I was totally relaxed. I was glad that I no longer let my asthma get in the way of what I wanted to do.

Now it's been five years since I made my resolution. I play outside with my little sister and I run laps in gym. I feel more laid back.

I also haven't had any asthma attacks in five years. This might be because I'm growing out of my asthma, which can happen sometimes, or maybe because I'm still careful to avoid things that trigger attacks.

I still get nervous sometimes when smoke blows into my face, and I never leave my house without my inhaler. But other than that, I'm fine. I've found ways to ensure that I have control of my asthma and not the other way around.

Looking back, I know I may have looked crazy doing things like crossing the street to avoid smokers and locking myself in the house. But I actually feel quite proud of myself for doing what I did. I was concerned for my health, and I took steps to take care of myself. I just went a little too far. Now that I've found my balance, all that's left to do is maintain it.

Viveca was 18 when she wrote this story.

How to Breathe Easier

By Natalie Olivero

With so many people in my neighborhood suffering from asthma, I wanted to learn more about the disease. So I interviewed Dr. Beverley J. Sheares, Associate Clinical Professor of Pediatrics at Columbia University. Dr. Sheares studies childhood asthma and environmental influences, and treats teens and children with asthma and other breathing problems.

NYC: What is asthma?

Dr. Beverley J. Sheares: Asthma is a condition in which the windpipe or airways become narrowed and results in people having difficulty breathing. The most common symptoms are wheezing, shortness of breath, chest tightness, and coughing.

NYC: What causes asthma?

Sheares: There are several risk factors for the development of asthma in young children. They include early exposure to environmental allergens (substances that cause allergic reactions, such as cockroaches, dust, and pet dander) and irritants such as tobacco smoke. Other risk factors include severe lower respiratory infections at an early age, rhinitis (runny nose without a cold), a parent or sibling with asthma, and eczema (skin rash).

NYC: What makes it worse?
Sheares: There are several things that trigger asthma. They include exposure to tobacco smoke, breathing cold air, viral infections, changes in weather or temperature, exercise, air pollution, allergens, strong odors from things like cologne, perfume and household cleaning products, and stress.

> Asthma is the most common childhood disease in the U.S.

NYC: What makes it better?
Sheares: Early and proper use of medications, and reduced exposure to things that trigger asthma.

NYC: Does it have a cure?
Sheares: There is no cure, but symptoms can be controlled with appropriate treatment. A person with asthma can live a normal life and participate in activities.

NYC: Is it possible for communities like East Harlem, New York (where I live) to get rid of asthma?
Sheares: It will be difficult to totally eradicate asthma because some of the susceptibility to asthma is genetic (it's passed down from parents to children).

NYC: How can you find out if you have asthma?
Sheares: If you have symptoms of asthma (cough, wheeze, shortness of breath, and chest tightness) after exposure to a trigger, you should tell a doctor or a nurse. There's also a breathing test called spirometry that can help confirm if you have asthma.

NYC: How serious a problem is asthma?
Sheares: Asthma is the most common chronic disease of childhood in the U.S. It's also the country's number one cause of school absences each year. It's estimated that 26.5 million

people in the U.S. have a diagnosis of asthma (nearly 6.1 million are under the age of 18).**

NYC: Do you have any advice for teens with asthma?
Sheares: It's important for teens to learn about their medications and take them without their parent's help. They need to learn the symptoms of asthma, and, specifically, their triggers, so they can reduce their exposure to them.

Patients with chronic or persistent asthma may not have symptoms every day, but they need to take medicine every day to keep their symptoms under control. They most certainly shouldn't smoke. This tip is good for all teens, whether they have asthma or not.

Natalie was 18 when she conducted this interview.

ARTHRITIS AT 13
By Chantel Morel

Every Friday in the ninth grade, my class went on trips around New York City. We'd visit the Brooklyn Bridge or other famous places, and those trips involved a lot of walking.

One Friday as we were waiting for the train at the beginning of the trip, I felt sharp pains in my back. They were so intense that they brought me to tears. I tried sitting, but it got worse. Not knowing what to do, I wandered away from the other kids, to the other end of the platform. I could hear my friends' cheerful voices, but they sounded far away. I could only think about the pain. I tried squeezing my back and hunching over, but it didn't go away.

By then these sudden pains had been happening for a little while, but I had no idea why; I just knew that it was starting to get in the way of my doing things. My teacher noticed and came over to ask what was wrong, but I just said that my back hurt. When I got home and changed, I noticed my knees were swollen and so were my ankles. This wasn't normal.

Nothing Serious

Soon after that field trip, my mother made an appointment for me with the pediatrician. My doctor couldn't tell what was wrong with me, so he sent me to a rheumatologist. I didn't know at the time what a rheumatologist is: a doctor who specializes in treating problems of the joints, muscles, and bones.

This one was based at New York Presbyterian Hospital in Washington Heights. His office was pretty and colorful, with a huge fish tank; there weren't many people there because my mom and I were extra early. I don't remember feeling especially nervous that morning; whatever was going on, I didn't think it could be very serious.

The doctor was nice. He touched all of my joints, bent my knees and elbows, made me squeeze his hand with my fingers, and looked at my ankles. He asked me where exactly I was getting pain.

Finally he said, "OK, so you definitely have arthritis." He said this very quickly, like it wasn't a big deal.

A Scary Word

My mom's expression didn't change; I guess it wasn't a surprise to her. It was a surprise to me, though. I thought arthritis was only for older people. I never imagined that arthritis might be the least of my worries.

"I'm almost 100% sure you have lupus, too," the doctor said next.

"What's that?" my mom asked.

"It's a disease similar to bone cancer," he explained. "If tests come back positive, I'd like to start a chemotherapy treatment as soon as possible."

When he said those words, I felt a knot sink down my throat. The world stopped for a second as I pictured myself bald, going through chemotherapy. I didn't look at my mom, as I knew she was terrified when she heard the word "cancer." On the outside I didn't show it, but I was terrified too.

The doctor said I needed a blood test to confirm it was lupus. I never had so much blood taken from me; I think they collected around nine tubes. I was even dizzy afterwards.

We left the building and walked back to the #1 train. "Ay, Dios mio, lupus, that's serious. Where in the world did this come from?" my mom said.

She wouldn't stop talking about chemotherapy all the way home. I could tell she was scared for me, and I didn't want to add to her stress.

Laughing It Off

I realized then that this meant being the brave one. Though I was scared, I told myself I was going to be fine. I tried to make it seem as if it didn't affect me and I joked about it: "Oh, my God, I'm an old lady already with arthritis," I said to my family when we got home.

Everyone laughed and it helped get the whole lupus thing out of their minds. If I showed that I was OK, I knew they would be OK. I felt that I could handle this; above all, I didn't want them to feel bad about it or get sad.

Two weeks later, the results came back. I didn't have lupus, just arthritis. I literally took a deep breath, enjoying my relief. For a while, I was so grateful I didn't have lupus that I didn't even care about having arthritis.

But once the idea of having lupus left my head and the arthritis pain continued, some of that strength and resolve I'd shown at first began to get shaky. It was difficult. I used to come home with swollen knees and ankles, and my back bothered me a lot, too. There was a point where some of the knuckles on my fingers started getting sort of bent and disfigured, which is normal with arthritis. I also started getting something called nodules, which were like tiny little bones popping out of the skin on my hands.

Even little things, like squeezing the toothpaste tube or opening a carton of juice, became difficult. I almost felt disabled, knowing that the simplest things in the world were things I could barely do anymore. It was hard feeling like I couldn't be normal and do things I used to.

Sorry Inside

It was especially hard for me to feel disabled because pretty much since the day I learned to walk, dancing has been my love and passion. I used to dance all the time—mainly hip-hop and some ballet—and I was really flexible. But the arthritis made it all harder. I couldn't do a lot of dances that I used to because it was too painful. I had trouble with moves that involved flexibility.

On the outside, I still seemed fine and I kept joking. I played around with the nodules on my hand in front of friends at school, moving my wrist around so you could see the funny-looking little bones sticking out. I wasn't ashamed; instead I embraced it, and made my family and friends laugh.

But inside, I was mad and sad to have this. I sometimes cried when I was by myself in my room or in the shower. I'd wonder, "Why me?" and think I was the only kid in the world with this. I didn't want anyone feeling sorry for me, but I guess what I was doing was even worse—I was feeling sorry for myself.

Almost Me

Over time, though, the things that I saw because I had this condition helped me learn to deal with it. The clinic I went to treated kids with arthritis and all sorts of other diseases. One day I saw an adorable little kid there with a mask on, and I learned she had cancer. I also saw a boy with liver problems who had a bag attached to his insides.

When I saw these kids, I thought, "Wow, these kids have more serious health problems than me and they still have smiles on their faces." I started to feel bad about feeling sorry for myself.

Meeting a girl the same age as me had the biggest impact. One day I was in the doctor's office and saw this girl with her mother. My mom and hers started talking.

"Hey," the girl said to me. "I'm Tiffany."

"I'm Chantel. So you have arthritis too?" I'd been over-hearing my mom talk with hers.

"Yeah, and lupus. I had chemotherapy but it's done now," she said. Wow, I thought. That was almost me.

What Arthritis?
We exchanged AIM names and contact info. I was interested in learning more about her and her story. We did stay in touch for a while, and I got to see that she didn't let her condition keep her from having a happy life. Even going through chemo hadn't ruined her outlook.

This was when I saw that I wasn't alone. Hearing Tiffany's story made me even more grateful for my health and more ready to enjoy life.

Soon, my clinic started mailing me invites to special events for kids with arthritis. Even though I couldn't attend any of these, I did research online and found out there are thousands of other teens out there with the same condition as me. I found it inspirational to read their stories and to see how they refused to let the disease get in their way or slow them down.

I decided I'd do the same: In every way possible, I would live my life as if I didn't have the disease. Yes, there were little things I couldn't do, but I decided not to let it get to me. I would focus on school and other things in my life. I would simply put arthritis out of my head.

Of course, I couldn't ignore it when I was going to physiotherapy. But I went to sessions with a positive attitude; I kept in mind that it would be good for me. It did help me, and it was even kind of fun at times. It involved a lot of special exercises that made my joints less stiff. Eventually, I completed the program and began taking medication to ease the pain.

Empathy and Strength
It's now been about four years since I was first diagnosed. I am glad to say I'm off medications and barely ever get pain. Arthritis isn't something that just goes away for good; it can get better, but I will always have it. Still, the doctor was

surprised by my improvement, since my condition was so bad at first. He was planning to start me on a stronger medicine, but I got better.

I'm happy I'm mostly pain-free, but I'm also grateful for this experience. I got to see what it's like to be a kid who is not in perfect health and now I can empathize with other kids. The experience made me appreciate my life and what I have more than I ever did before.

Having a disease at a young age can make you stronger. There were times at first when I was sad and felt like giving up, but seeing how many other kids are going through illness helped me persevere. So if you ever have a medical condition, I would say: Don't feel like you're alone in the world. Don't feel ashamed. There are other people out there you can talk to, and knowing you're not alone can make a big difference.

The Junior Arthritis Alliance, part of the Arthritis Foundation, provides information and resources for people with Juvenile Arthritis and their families. (They also organize an annual nationwide Juvenile Arthritis Conference.) To learn more, visit arthritis.org/ja-alliance-main.php or call the New York chapter of the Arthritis Foundation at 1-212-984-8700. For information and resources on lupus, visit the website of Lupus Alliance of America, lupusalliance.org.

MY LIFE WITH OCD

By Anonymous

Voices coming from our garden woke me in the middle of the night. I heard a car door open, and someone putting suitcases in the trunk. I looked out the window and saw my father getting in his friend's blue car. I ran outside; I only had a moment to hug him. I had known he was leaving our home in Istanbul, Turkey, to get a job in the United States, but it didn't hit me that he was really leaving until then. I was 6 years old.

My father was leaving my mother, my brother, and me to go to New York. He told me he'd be back with Barbie dolls. I didn't know he'd be gone for five years.

My father had had a successful business importing electronics from the U.S. and selling them in Turkey. He had built the business over many years, but his partner stole a lot of money from him. So my father moved to New York City to find work, but all he could get was a job driving a taxi.

I missed him and dreamed about having him back. At school, I felt like an outsider whenever we got report cards. My friends' fathers and mothers were there to congratulate them, but I only had my mother.

It was also hard to see my mom try to handle everything on her own. My older brother was moody and difficult and I complained a lot about missing my father. I sometimes heard her crying in the bathroom. I wished my father would come back.

Two years later, three of my grandparents died within a few months of one another. Soon after that, we almost lost our house due to some illegality with our mortgage contract. My mother worked it out with a lawyer but, for a few months, she was stressed out all the time. Even though she never took it out on me or my brother, I found myself worrying about her a lot.

Too Much at Once

All of these things happened one after another over five years. I started to develop irrational fears about my family and concerns about needing to stay safe. For instance, when I was 11, I would touch the floor and think that I might get an infection from those germs. Then I'd be convinced that those germs would pass to my family, so I would wash my hands three times in a row, because I'd heard that Allah's lucky number is three. Sometimes that would happen every day.

I thought doing this would prevent anyone in my family from dying, or being sad, sick, or separated from us.

I also feared that a stranger would break into our house. So before I went to sleep, I would go into each room and pray three times. That would help reduce my fear. I would put a chair in front of the front door so if somebody tried to break in, I would hear them. I also slept in my mom's bed with her because I was having nightmares about losing my dad.

I didn't know it at the time, but I was developing obsessive-compulsive disorder (OCD), a mental illness that causes you to have "obsessions" (recurrent thoughts) and/or "compulsions" (impulses to do things over and over). Even though you know they are excessive, you can't stop.

Stressed and Anxious

This constant obsessive thinking and compulsive behavior made me stressed and anxious. I knew this was all in my mind but I couldn't control it.

A year later, when I was almost 12, we were all able to join my father in New York City. But after a month, I was diagnosed with scoliosis, a condition where your spine curves into either an "S" or "C" shape.

I had to have surgery to correct it, which was successful. But while I was recovering I became preoccupied with my health because I had to be careful about my movements while my back was healing. I was also stuck in the house bored for three months with not much to distract me, so my obsessive thoughts took hold.

One day, for instance, I saw a pimple on my lip, immediately Googled "pimple on lip," and read I might have lip cancer. I got so upset my mom had my aunts and uncles call me to reassure me that I was perfectly healthy. These kinds of recurrent, worrisome, obsessive thoughts are part of having OCD.

Find Me a Doctor!
One night, I felt like I was in a locked box and I couldn't get out. I went to my mom and dad and said, "I need a therapist!"

"We know you've been through a big surgery and that's normal for you to be scared, but why do you think you need therapy?" they asked.

"I feel like these constant scary thoughts are taking over me," I said. "I am not myself. I want the old me back."

A month later, my dad found me a psychiatrist. I was late for my first appointment because having OCD makes it difficult for me to be ready at a specific time. I couldn't touch a lot of things without washing my hands over and over, not even myself, because even though my mom cleaned the house every day, I only saw germs and disease.

I cried a lot when I met my doctor and it felt so good to say everything that was buried inside of me. He told me I had OCD and what that was. He said I may have developed it because I had a past with hard times piled on top of one another. People who have experienced childhood trauma have an increased risk of developing OCD. It can also be inherited.

The psychiatrist put me on the anti-depressant medication Zoloft. After a few weeks, I started feeling better. It didn't make me forget about OCD thoughts, but it made me calmer and my thoughts less intense, so I had more control over them.

Seventh grade started soon after and school seemed cleaner to me than home. I was comfortable there. Maybe it was because of the medication, or maybe it was because I was reunited with my friends again so I actually had something else to think about rather than OCD thoughts.

Getting Better, With Setbacks

In each session, the psychiatrist asked me what I was afraid of. Then he'd come up with a strategy to help me overcome the particular fear. For instance, I told him I was scared of touching the subway poles because I see that everybody touches them and think they must be full of germs.

"You are right," he'd say. "But how about if you touch it for a second and then you clean your hands? Trust me, once you do that you will realize that yes, you do get germs, but the soap kills them."

"OK, I'll try."

The next time I got on the train I looked at the subway pole as I sat down. Then, I got up and touched it for a second. But then I thought, "Wow, I was scared of this?" Then I touched it again and again.

Once I arrived at school, I told myself not to go to the bathroom to wash my hands, and I was able to do that. I didn't think about this for the rest of the day and don't even remember if I washed my hands when I got home.

I Am Doing My Best

The next time I was with my psychiatrist, I was very excited to tell him that I touched the subway pole.

"It took me 15 minutes to be able to touch it, and I didn't feel the need to wash my hands afterward."

"Very good! Next time, try to touch it after only 10 minutes," he said.

The doctor also had me write down everything I was afraid of, how much it bothered me on a scale of 1 to 10, if I overcame the fear, and if so, how long it took. He also wanted me to record if I washed my hands afterwards, among other observations.

I wasn't successful every time. OCD doesn't always have the same intensity. Sometimes I feel good and can control my compulsive behavior. But other days it holds me back from doing what I'm capable of and that really hurts.

About six months after I started therapy, I was late to a math test. That day my obsessive thoughts kept on coming to my mind and bothering me while I was taking the test. I wrote all of my answers three times hoping that would help me erase bad thoughts I have like dying, having a disease, or losing someone I love. I got a bad grade because I took too long, ran out of time, and couldn't finish. I went to the bathroom and cried without any sound because it was too much.

Learning to Live With It
Now it's been four years since I started therapy and medication and I'm still trying to learn how to live with OCD. I know how to handle it much better, but there are times when it all comes back. Sometimes I feel like my family expects me to be cured. I wish it was that easy to get over it. But I believe I can never beat OCD because it's part of me.

I wanted to write this story to give people an idea of what having OCD is like. I am not always able to push away my obsessive thoughts. I want people to understand that when this happens, I need their support instead of them telling me, "How could you not do it?" Saying those things makes me feel weak. Instead I want to hear, "It's OK. I know you are doing your best." And that's it.

Worst. Year. Ever. My Struggle with Scoliosis

By Hande Erkan

When I was 11, I moved from Turkey to New York. After a month I was just starting to get used to my new school and make friends.

One day, I reached forward to put an apple onto my tray when a pain shot through my upper back below my shoulder, as if someone had stabbed me. It hurt a lot, but I tried to quietly calm myself. I was shy and I didn't want anybody to pay attention to me.

I spent the afternoon massaging to my back. I knew something was wrong, but I assumed I'd just slept in the wrong position.

That night, the pain got worse. I asked my mom to massage my back. When she took off my shirt she said in alarm, "What is this?" She said that my back looked crooked. How had this happened?

A Scary Diagnosis
The next day I found out that I had scoliosis, a condition in which your spine curves into an "S" or "C" shape. Most people

have a little curve, but people with scoliosis have more than a 10-degree curve. Severe scoliosis can even be life-threatening because the curved spine could affect your organs—for example, pushing on your lungs and making it hard to breathe.

There's no good time to get a serious condition like scoliosis, but it happened at one of the most difficult points of my life. I was 11, trying to fit into a new country. I didn't know the language well, which made it hard to make friends and keep up my grades. My parents were struggling financially after this big move, so I'd gone from living in a big house in Turkey to a one-room apartment. On top of all that, I'd just started my period.

A week later, we went to the hospital to get X-rays that would tell us how serious my scoliosis was. While waiting for the results, I tried to prepare myself for the possible outcomes: either I would have to wear a brace, or I would need surgery to fix the curve in my spine. Surgery seemed scary. But if I had to wear a brace, would people notice it? Would it be uncomfortable?

I found out that my spine had a 45-degree curve already and that I needed surgery. I started crying. I asked my mom why we'd come to New York. I was blaming New York for my scoliosis. I thought if I had stayed in Istanbul, I would not have this illness, I would not have my period, I would live in my beautiful house, have all my friends and family close by, and be a normal 11-year-old girl.

"You should feel lucky that you are here because imagine how much this surgery would have cost us in Turkey—we wouldn't have been able to afford it," my mom said.

As upset as I was, I knew she was right.

Trying to Be Brave
That evening my family went grocery shopping, but I wanted to stay alone at home. I went on Google and watched scoliosis surgery videos. I didn't get scared. Watching the surgeries

actually encouraged me to be brave. I decided that I would not show my family that I was scared, so they could also be brave and strong.

It took several months to schedule the surgery. During that time my spine's curve increased from 45 to 65 degrees, which was bad for my health. I couldn't participate in gym class, and whenever I went to dance class my back would hurt. I got tired easily.

Other people started noticing. Almost everyday someone asked me why I stood and walked with my left shoulder bent. It made me feel insecure. Sometimes I would say, "Mind your own business." Other times I was more patient and I would explain scoliosis to them.

It felt uncomfortable to share this personal information all the time. I hated it when people reacted with pity. It made me feel weak when I was trying so hard to be strong and brave.

Surgery Time
Finally it was time for me to prepare for surgery. I met my surgeon, Dr. Lonner, who seemed to genuinely care about me and understand what I was going through, not only physically but psychologically. He told my parents, "Don't worry, your daughter will be my daughter during those eight hours of surgery, and she will come out a healthy, beautiful young girl." His honesty and confidence made me feel even braver and much more secure.

By the day of my surgery, my spine was 75 degrees curved. At the hospital, I tried to pretend like it was a normal morning. A lot of my family members were there with me. My aunt even came from Turkey to support me. While I waited for the hospital staff to call my name, I was laughing, smiling, and trying to ignore the fact that Dr. Lonner would soon be cutting into my back.

But when they called my name and I started changing into a blue surgery gown and socks, it hit me, and I began to cry in front of my mom. Then I saw my dad crying. I realized that all of us had been holding in our tears to be ready for this day.

They lay me down on the gurney to take me to surgery. My mom was also dressed in a blue surgical gown so she could walk with me to the operating room. I was OK until I arrived in the operating room. It was huge. I saw the surgical tools and there were many doctors and helpers. I saw the bags of blood that my mom and dad donated in case something went wrong during surgery and I needed a transfusion.

I held my mom's hand and started crying loudly. It was so scary. I'll never forget how, after they gave me the shot of anesthesia, my mom told me "I love you" with tears in her eyes. After that, everything went black.

The surgery went well. On the second day, I was allowed to get up and walk, which sounds so easy but it was like a new experience. When I stood up I felt the weight of the 17 pieces of metal that the doctors had put on my spine to keep it straight. It was worse when they asked me to walk.

Totally Dependent
I had physical therapy for two days to help me practice walking, climbing steps, lying down, and other everyday activities. All four days I spent in the hospital, my entire family was there to support me.

For the next three months, I depended on my mom for everything. She had to lay me down on my bed and help me shift from one side to the other. She'd pull me up and take me to the bathroom. She had to wash me since I wasn't even able to raise my arms. Bathing was complicated; I had to wear a garbage bag to keep my surgery wound clean and dry while it healed.

I was isolated. I couldn't go outside because what if somebody accidentally pushed me? Plus, I was tired most of the time. That summer my friends would go to the beach and I felt sad and lonely.

I was also preoccupied about illness, which I guess was a psychological effect of scoliosis. One day I found a pimple on my lip and I searched on Google about it and decided I might have a lip cancer. "Let's go to the doctor to make sure, Dad," I pleaded. My mom was having back pain from pulling me up, and I started searching Google for back diseases she might have.

I got tired of these negative thoughts. This wasn't me; I was normally an optimistic girl. So one night I told my parents I need a therapist. Their first reaction was "Why?" But after I explained, they understood.

Therapy Eased My Fears

I was lucky: My middle school counselor found a good Turkish therapist in Manhattan. We connected because we shared a cultural background. This also allowed my mom to talk to the therapist since she didn't speak English as well as she does now.

During my recovery, I was so desperate to dance again. Dancing is my passion; I've been doing it since I was small. When I dance, I find myself at peace. Not being able to dance made me feel that I couldn't express my feelings.

Three months after surgery, I was able to raise my arms, take a shower by myself, and do daily life skills and movements. However, I wasn't feeling ready to dance. I was afraid of getting hurt.

My therapist helped. When I told him I was afraid of getting hurt because I lose myself when I dance, he said, "So what? Life is all about falling and getting right back up and moving forward. What if you had a minor car accident? Does that mean you would never ever again drive a car?"

With the help of therapy I started to dance again and feel less worried about getting another serious illness.

Making Good Out of Bad
I'm now a junior in high school and I feel strong in my body as well as my mind. I am thankful for being healthy. I don't take my health for granted, and I try to take care of myself. I've also learned to have empathy and patience for people who suffer from illnesses and disabilities.

Scoliosis has helped me be prepared for the unexpected and given me the confidence to persevere no matter what happens. Now I believe in the saying "Everything has something good and bad in it." Sometimes bad moments in life help us learn to stand on our feet to confront problems and be more ambitious about our goals and dreams. That's where I find myself now.

HANDBALL TAKES AWAY MY TROUBLES

By Cynthia Orbes

When I go to the handball courts, it's like I'm entering a different world where I can escape my anger and confusion and have fun. I want to win, so when I enter the courts I have to throw away all of my thoughts and focus on the game.

I play handball at a park near where I live. In summer the courts are always crowded, even though there are 12 courts at that park. In the winter it's dead silent and you can't find anyone to play with. Maybe one or two people are practicing, at most (one of them just might be me).

It's hard to play in the cold because it hurts when the ball hits your palm, but sometimes I make exceptions, like when I really want to play badly and the courts are clean. Sometimes I even play in the rain. Still, the sun goes down at around 4:30 so I can't play too long. And I really can't play in snow. I would probably break my leg.

So in winter I can't wait for spring when I can play again. When I go back to the courts, I feel reborn and energized, like a mummy that has just woken up from 1,000 years of rest.

I first started going to the handball courts when I was about 13. Until then, handball wasn't my thing. I liked hanging on the park's swings with my good friend Lauren, singing rock songs.

When I was 10, I saw a friend's sister play and I decided to learn because it looked fun. I tried but then I gave up. It was too hard for me. I guess I was too young. She tried to teach me and I just didn't get it.

Then, when I turned 13, I tried again and I was determined. I wanted to learn badly. I practiced alone, throwing the ball to the wall and trying to catch it, then throwing the ball and trying to hit it. I would always miss the ball or it would go out of the court, but the more I practiced, the better my aim got and the harder I hit it.

Then I started to play with a friend. It took about a year to become good. It's not easy at the beginning. You have to remember the rules and learn the cool moves, like the killer, roller, cutting the ball, or doing a backhand.

> Handball takes my mind away from my troubles.

To play you need power, placement, agility, and precision. You need power because if you're tired you won't be able to run for the ball, and if you don't hit the ball hard enough, then your ball probably won't make the wall and your opponent will win a point.

Placement means thinking about where the other person will hit the ball and getting ready to run there. If you're not in the right spot, it'll be hard to hit it back.

That's when you need to be quick. Otherwise, your opponent will ace you (that's when someone serves the ball so fast to the opposite side from where you're standing that you miss it). You need to be precise when you hit the ball, to make sure it bounces as far from your opponent as possible.

To do all of these things well, I need to concentrate. That's why handball takes my mind away from my troubles.

For me, the handball courts are a good place to get away from everything and escape reality. When I'm angry, playing alone relieves my anger. I hit the ball hard and quickly. If I'm mad at a particular person, then I picture smacking them while I'm playing, instead of doing it in real life.

When I do good moves like a roller or killer, I know I'm doing a good job and that makes me feel better. If I keep missing the ball or if it goes in the wrong direction, I get pissed off. But either way, I just like to see if I'm getting better. I'm always up for a good challenge.

Cynthia was 15 when she wrote this story. She later attended John Jay College.

How Exercise Relieves Stress

By Nakese Bullock

Research has found that exercise helps people cope better with stress and feel more confident. Researchers don't exactly understand how exercise helps a person feel better. But people who exercise feel less anxious or depressed than people who don't exercise, some studies have found.

One explanation is that when people exercise, their bodies release endorphins, chemicals that make a person temporarily feel better. Other researchers think that exercise helps the body's central nervous system communicate better with the rest of the body, which can make a person feel better in general.

Some say there's a strong connection between the body and the mind—if you do something good for the body, they say, your mind might also feel more at ease.

Whatever the reason for it, exercising for as little as twenty minutes a day may help a person manage stress and feel better.

It's better to choose an exercise activity that gets the heart pumping faster than normal, like jogging or aerobics, but just walking may help. However, you may not see results right away. It can take a few weeks to start getting the "feel-good" effects of exercise.

Nakese was 16 when she wrote this story.

YOGA RELAXES ME
By Niya Wilson

For a while, I was bummed out and I couldn't find a solution to my problems. My grades were slipping and my friends were truly being annoying.

I tried facing my problems head on by actually going to class and telling my friends to shut up. I also tried putting my problems behind me by leaving my friends alone and avoiding them. None of that worked. Actually, it stressed me out even more.

Then my know-it-all friend told me about yoga. She said, "Yoga is the greatest way to relieve stress." Of course, being the Doubting Thomas that I am, I thought she was totally out of her mind.

She does her yoga exercises all the time, and she always does this chanting thing and massages her face in circular motions. I said to myself, "I couldn't be seen doing something like that."

To try to get me involved in yoga, she said, "See how happy I am doing yoga? I'm more relaxed and stress free. You could be, too!" She said it with every inch of her pride.

"Yeah, right," I said. How could being "one with myself" be healthy? It sounded crazy to me.

Her nagging and her pleading made me even more stressed. As you can see, I get stressed a lot! I'm such a baby when I don't get my way. But I finally gave in and did some yoga exercises with her and, truthfully, I liked it a lot.

This is what we did. First, my friend lit scented candles to give the room a peaceful atmosphere. Second, I sat Indian-style on the floor and took deep breaths to clear my mind of all thoughts.

> I realized that I was making my problems bigger than they were.

Clearing my head was kind of hard, since everything my life depended on was on my mind. But I sat in silence and relaxed, and that made it all clear.

While sitting in silence, I stretched a little to make my body as relaxed as my mind. Eventually, I couldn't think of anything.

Then, before I left this new relaxed world, I prayed—not only for myself, but for my family and friends (and even a few enemies).

After I opened my eyes I felt much calmer and I thought through my problems again. I realized that I was making my problems bigger than they were. I also knew my attitude had to change and that I had to start to get to know who I was and keep myself from doing things that I knew were not me.

I really liked the calm feeling of doing yoga with my friend and I got more curious about it. So when my teacher gave me a flyer for a local yoga center, I decided that I wanted to take a professional yoga class.

The night before the big class I was excited and a little nervous. I had butterflies in my stomach. I wasn't sure what to expect.

It took me a while to figure out exactly where the place was, but I left home so early that I got there when it was still closed. Class started at 9:45 a.m. and I was there at 8:21. While waiting for the doors to open, I tried to imagine what was inside.

I visualized a big room with candles and encouraging posters and pictures on the walls, saying things like, "Reach for the love within, it's the only way to peace and serenity."

I imagined massage tables and a teacher with a very soft voice. She would walk very gracefully, like she could just glide through the world.

I woke up to reality when the doors opened. The place wasn't what I expected. It was small and very plain, with a black sheet covering the front entrance to block out any "peeping Toms" who wanted to be nosy. There weren't any massage tables or posters and pictures around. I laughed at my imagination. The teacher wasn't what I imagined her to be, either. She was loud and stomped when she walked. When I introduced myself to her, she was cheerful, bubbly, and very nice. Because I couldn't do any exercises in my street clothes, I went to the bathroom to change into sweats.

When I walked out of the bathroom, the door to the main room was locked. I began to bang on it. Not one soul heard me, and I was getting mad until the teacher said, "Where's Niya? Oh, my, the door must have locked on her."

> It seemed really weird to be chanting. I felt like I was in a cult.

When she opened the door, my embarrassment grew as I stepped into the room and the other yoga students, all adults, were staring at me.

The class began. I had no idea what I was doing, so I copied what I saw. I went and picked up a mat to place it on the floor. I sat on the mat and the teacher started speaking in a totally different language. Then she told us to cross our legs Indian-style, close our eyes, and repeat after her. She continued in a chant.

To me, it seemed really weird to be chanting. I felt like I was in a cult where everyone did the same thing, the same way. After the chant, there was complete silence for maybe one minute. I couldn't help but open my eyes and glance at the other students. They were all perfectly still. They looked as though they already had taken this beginners' course. The teacher spoke, so I quickly closed my eyes.

She instructed us to go get a belt (really, a long piece of thick fabric) and said, "Put the belt over your shoulder." I totally thought this was weird. I had to put my right arm over my right shoulder, and my left arm under my left shoulder, holding the belt behind my back.

Holding this position, I had to push my chest up, stretching my front and back muscles. After standing in position for a moment (it was hard!), the teacher told us to exhale out of the stretch.

During this exercise, the teacher said a lot of strange phrases, like "Let your face feel like butter" and "Stretch your body like a playful cat who has just woken up to a warm glass of milk." To me her phrases were weird but humorous. They helped me to relax.

The rest of the exercises were pretty much the same: stretching and breathing. It sounds simple, but the way we had to hold the positions was really hard and, by the end, my muscles hurt.

My favorite exercise was the very last one. We each lay on top of a blanket, which had two blankets on top supporting our heads. I also had a round pillow for my back. I lay completely still with my chest sticking out. The teacher told us to close our eyes and "be one with ourselves."

While laying there the teacher put a blanket over me (well, not just me, but the entire class). Her next instructions were to "relax and take everything off your mind. Concentrate on yourself, nothing else."

She continued to say this until I drifted off. I didn't think I was asleep because I still heard her talking, but I felt like I was in my own world.

When the class was over, I felt kind of tired and calm. It was a little strange, but I liked it.

In the beginning, I was definitely skeptical. Giving yoga a chance made me see how taking time to stretch and relax could give me a new way to handle stress. It gave me quiet time to be with myself and God.

Like me, most teens are faced with many stressful situations, and we don't know how to go about dealing with stress. So we settle for not handling the situation or for handling it without thinking of the consequences. Yoga is something to try—it can calm you down and clear your head.

Niya was 18 when she wrote this story.

Poetry Keeps Me Calm

By Ashunte Hunt

When I was 14, I was put in my first group home. I was facing many struggles at that time. I was still grieving for my parents, who had died when I was younger, and I was living with a stepmom who abused me. I also had to deal with bullying from my peers in middle school.

I was caught in a circle of abuse. I'd get beat up in school, and then I would go home and go through the beatings that my stepmom called "discipline." When I was put in the group home, I had to deal with a whole new situation all by myself, so I got really stressed out.

I had no way to express my feelings because I wouldn't talk to anybody. I didn't trust them. Not being able to express my feelings gave me no choice but to keep them bottled up inside, and the more I bottled up my feelings, the more likely I was to explode. My anger kept rising and rising, and then I'd get into fights or vandalize property. I always had evil thoughts in my head.

looked at the world as if everybody was against me. I hated everyone I didn't know, and I grew very skeptical around

140

the people that I did know. And if I felt that I was being disrespected in any way, I just started flipping like I was crazy.

I was my own Jekyll and Hyde—in certain situations I could control myself, but when someone provoked me I felt powerless to stop myself from going off on them. The people that pushed me to snap were the people that bullied me, made fun of my circumstances, and tried to play me like I was soft.

When I got mad in my group home, I turned into a demolition man. I demolished furniture, couches, chairs, walls, and my room. I also picked fights whenever people pushed my buttons.

One day in my group home the barber came through and I decided to get my hair cut. As I was waiting for my turn, I went downstairs and started playing a pinball game on the computer.

> When I started to feel angry, I'd write a poem or two.

One of my peers came downstairs to tell me that it was my turn to get my hair cut. He tried to get me to go upstairs by turning off the computer screen. I turned it back on. I thought he was playing at first, so I didn't get mad or take it seriously.

He did it again and I turned it back on to continue playing. I started to get agitated. If my anger was a pot of water on the stove, it was just starting to bubble.

When he did it the third time, I turned it back on and told him, "If you turn off the computer screen again I will hurt you!" This time I was mad—the water was about to boil over.

Then he did it again. I was in a rage. We started fighting, we got a couple of hits in, then staff came to break it up.

I had so much anger in me at my group home that I didn't really want to deal with anything that anybody wanted me to do. But one day my favorite group home staff let me listen to his Tupac and Eminem CDs. When I listened to Tupac and Eminem, I felt this unique feeling that no other artists gave me.

When I listened to Tupac's music, I got the message of street life and family problems. When I listened to Eminem's music, I felt the anger and rage that I'd been through. That's when the next stage opened up for me.

I was listening to one of Eminem's CDs when this one song caught my attention. It was titled "Rock Bottom," and the song was about how life can really push you to the edge and bring you down.

The first line pulled me in: "I feel like I'm walkin' a tightrope without a circus net." I related to that line because the lifestyle that I was going through made me feel like I was walking that tightrope. So I decided to write something of my own, and I got a piece of paper and a pencil.

In that first poem I expressed my built-up anger, rage, and depression. I didn't feel anything while I wrote it. But a week later I caught the feelings after reading it over and over again.

I called my first poem "Will somebody referee this fight I'm fighting?" One of the lines was: "I wouldn't care if the grim reaper reap, cause my life is something that I now don't want to keep." And that line alone hit me so hard that I had to dig into myself and see what would make me write that, because I really didn't recall writing it. That's when I realized how much pain I was in and how much I needed to release all my stress.

So I started writing more poetry. The poems that I wrote in my group home were about me, my anger, depression, stress, and any other thing that bothered me. When I wrote poetry it was like I could just write forever to express my feelings, as long as I had enough paper and lead to do so.

The poetry affected my anger a little at a time. When I started to feel angry, I'd write a poem or two to release my feelings before I did something that I'd regret. I'd still be angry, but I could at least let some of it out before it got out of hand.

When I found out that my first love had cheated on me, I wanted to chop her head off. Her love was priceless and I felt she threw my heart in the trash. I was so angry that I had to release my anger or I would have ended up in jail. So the first thing I did was write two poems. Then, when I saw her, I was able to stay calm even though it still hurt.

When I read over my poems I can acknowledge my feelings, and that helps me think about what I can do to make the situation better. I ask myself how I can do something different to avoid getting physical or making myself a threat to anybody.

> Writing my feelings taught me to look at the world differently.

I didn't get into that many fights after I started writing poetry, but I really can't say that it put an end to the fighting either. Sometimes I feel like going back to my old behaviors when I get mad because I still have a lot of anger inside of me. Certain situations give me flashbacks of how I would react if I were the old me.

I will still fight someone for disrespecting the memory of my mother and father, or for threatening me or my space. But it's been four or five months since I had my last fight.

And the last time I demolished something was a year ago. I was angry at my ex-girlfriend because we got into an argument over the phone, and I demolished my bowling trophy and some things that she had given me. I'll only demolish something now if I'm so upset that poetry can't help me.

Poetry can't help me get over the abuse I've been through or the fact that my parents are gone. I have to reach deep down inside to recover from those things, and even though poetry helps me get in touch with my inside, it doesn't cover those subjects. It might help numb it at times, but it doesn't hit the spot like I want it to.

But writing my feelings down on paper taught me how to look at the world differently. My temper has calmed down, and I don't feel powerless over my behaviors anymore. I feel like a real human being who can civilize himself and cool off on his own.

Ashunte was 17 when he wrote this story. He attended Schenectady County Community College.

Do for You

By Shanté Brown

Relax. Read. Do some writing. Take a long walk. Have a good laugh. Do some crying. Pick up a Bible. Reflect on who you are. Envision who you want to be. Pamper yourself. Do what you want to do, for once, instead of doing what is expected of you.

These are all ways to increase your sense of self and gain inner strength.

Music can help. So can silence. Thinking also works, but sometimes it's best not to think. The important thing is to take some time out for you, to concentrate on you as a person.

Do whatever works for you—for me, writing, music, and aromatherapy are the major things that help me to relax and get in touch with myself.

When I get the urge, I just take out my journal and start to write. Some days I free-write, so I can get all my thoughts across without having to worry about making sense.

Free-writing is my favorite form of writing because I can take all the time I need and write however many pages I want about whatever comes into my head. Whatever is on my mind, getting it out of my head and onto paper is a great stress reliever.

> Do some writing.
> Take a long walk.
> Have a good laugh.

Some days I decide that I want to get in a poetry mood. This is my next favorite type of writing and for me this comes as a gift. As much as I love to write, I also enjoy being unique, and my poetry is one way that I can satisfy that desire.

Scented candles usually burn as I write (that's where the aromatherapy comes in) and my radio is always on. This relaxes me. Some days, instead of writing, I'll dance in front of my mirror.

Sometimes I just try to get my feelings out. I cry or I try to have a good laugh. This depends on what type of mood I'm in. All of these things help me find peace of mind because they are the things I feel most comfortable doing.

Some days I'll talk to my grandmother, who is now in heaven. Other days I'll say a prayer to God. Sometimes I write the prayers down so I can get a lot more off my mind.

Alone in my room, music playing, candles burning, writing, dancing, or praying, this is for me and no one else. Doing these things, I get a better understanding of myself.

Shanté was 17 when she wrote this story. She majored in English and elementary education at Russell Sage College.

NATURE IS MY SALVATION

By Emily Orchier

Have you ever been so depressed that you can't sleep? (Too unhappy.) You also can't eat. (There's never anything good in the house, and even if there were, it would be tasteless.) You can't read (no attention span). You have no friends to call up on the phone, nothing good on TV. So you sigh, press your face down harder into your pillow, lament, and shed a few tears.

This was my life two years ago. I had just turned 14 and I felt bleak. As I lay in my bed one Saturday, my mother peeked into my room to make her regular "is Em still alive?" check. Even I knew that if I spent much more time like this, she would have to begin dusting me.

"Hi, hon," my mom said. I grunted in acknowledgment. "How are you feeling today, sweetheart?" she asked. "How do you think?" I replied sarcastically.

After suggesting a number of things for me to do (that were promptly rejected), my mother made her move:

"Emily! Get dressed! I'm taking the dog out for a walk, and you are coming with me!"

"Why?" I moaned.

"Because it will make you feel better."

147

The thought of moving was unbearable. I felt as if I all of my body parts were weighed down by a ton of bricks. I couldn't remember the last time I had gone outside. Somehow I found the strength to slip on a pair of blue jeans and a black sweatshirt. My mother was waiting at the door for me, leash and dog in hand.

"I still don't get how going for a walk will make me feel any better," I complained.

My mother gave me a look and opened the door. We stepped outside. It was one of those unusually warm March days when you could get away with jeans and a sweatshirt, but the signs of spring had yet to appear. It had been a long time since the warmth of the sun had touched my cheeks.

> I couldn't remember the last time I had gone outside.

My mother led the dog and me to The Aqueduct, a dirt path that historically carried water underground to a nearby city. Now its sole purpose is for outdoor recreation. I carried on and complained throughout the entire excursion.

"I'm tired! This is boring, mother. When can we go home?"

"Not just yet," she'd say.

My mother stopped to say "hi" to every jogger, dog-walker, runner, and bicyclist who passed us by. Sometimes she would get into a conversation with someone. She exerted herself—made herself happier than I knew she felt from being around me. They would talk about the weather, dogs, and other topics of small talk. I thought it was all so senseless.

After walking for what seemed to be an eternity, my mother finally said that it was time to turn around. She was glowing.

When we got home, I was confronted with a new sensation. It was as if the ton of bricks had been lifted off my heart. But I didn't let this feeling last long, because I didn't know how to handle it. For nearly a year I had been immersed in sadness. How could I learn to feel happy again?

I soon found myself back in my room, in a comfortable funk. But that walk had done something to me. I didn't know how or why, but for a moment in time life almost felt all right. A week went by, and a new Saturday found me asking my mother if we could go for another walk.

April arrived, and with it an array of beautiful spring blossoms. I began to take my dog out for her mid-morning walks. We would go across the street to a big field, which led to small paths lined with daffodils, which in turn led to orchards with apple blossoms.

> For a moment in time life almost felt all right.

Smaller fields abounded with blooming dogwood and magnolia trees, and scattered patches of tiny purple wildflowers. Walking there, I was overcome by beautiful fragrances. It became my little slice of heaven. I was healing.

So it came to pass that I was the official dog walker of the family. Walking became an everyday affair for me, and I began to acknowledge the powerful solace that it brought me.

Late that summer, I remembered a small pond that my parents used to take me to when I was a very small child. Halsey Pond was its name. One morning I decided to make the trek over to Halsey.

It was very long for a walk, taking more than two hours to get there and back. But as soon as I laid eyes on the place, I knew that I loved it. Everywhere I looked, there was life—ducks, geese, deer, turkeys, water snakes, turtles, squirrels, and giant carp. I began to wake up early in the morning to take my daily pilgrimage there.

If walking was my spiritual practice, then Halsey was a wonderful sanctuary. I felt such peace and serenity while I was there. I also made many friends at the pond, and greeted every jogger, runner, dog-walker, or bicyclist who came my way.

My depression lifted in time. Now that I have been feeling so much better, I also have become much busier and have less time to walk. I no longer walk to Halsey Pond every morning. But I do make sure that I get out every day, if only for a little while. Walking was my salvation from the throes of depression. It is strong medicine for the soul.

Emily was 16 when she wrote this story.

Using the Book

Teens:
How to Get More Out of This Book

Self-help: The teens who wrote the stories in this book did so because they hope that telling their stories will help readers who are facing similar challenges. They want you to know that you are not alone, and that taking specific steps can help you manage or overcome very difficult situations. They've done their best to be clear about the actions that worked for them so you can see if they'll work for you.

Writing: You can also use the book to improve your writing skills. Each teen in this book wrote 5-10 drafts of his or her story before it was published. If you read the stories closely you'll see that the teens work to include a beginning, a middle, and an end, and good scenes, description, dialogue, and anecdotes (little stories). To improve your writing, take a look at how these writers construct their stories. Try some of their techniques in your own writing.

Resources on the Web

We will occasionally post Think About It questions on our website, www.youthcomm.org, to accompany stories in this and other Youth Communication books. We try out the questions with teens and post the ones they like best. Many teens report that writing answers to those questions in a journal is very helpful.

HOW TO USE THIS BOOK IN STAFF TRAINING

Staff say that reading these stories gives them greater insight into what teens are thinking and feeling, and new strategies for working with them. You can help the staff you work with by using these stories as case studies.

Select one story to read in the group, and ask staff to identify and discuss the main issue facing the teen. There may be disagreement about this, based on the background and experience of staff. That is fine. One point of the exercise is that teens have complex lives and needs. Adults can probably be more effective if they don't focus too narrowly and can see several dimensions of their clients.

Ask staff: What issues or feelings does the story provoke in them? What kind of help do they think the teen wants? What interventions are likely to be most promising? Least effective? Why? How would you build trust with the teen writer? How have other adults failed the teen, and how might that affect his or her willingness to accept help? What other resources would be helpful to this teen, such as peer support, a mentor, counseling, family therapy, etc?

Resources on the Web

From time to time we will post Think About It questions on our website, www.youthcomm.org, to accompany stories in this and other Youth Communication books. We try out the questions with teens and post the ones that they find most effective. We'll also post lessons for some of the stories. Adults can use the questions and lessons in workshops.

Teachers & Staff: How to Use This Book in Groups

When working with teens individually or in groups, you can use these stories to help young people face difficult issues in a way that feels safe to them. That's because talking about the issues in the stories usually feels safer to teens than talking about those same issues in their own lives. Addressing issues through the stories allows for some personal distance; they hit close to home, but not too close. Talking about them opens up a safe place for reflection. As teens gain confidence talking about the issues in the stories, they usually become more comfortable talking about those issues in their own lives.

Below are general questions to guide your discussion. In most cases you can read a story and conduct a discussion in one 45-minute session. Teens are usually happy to read the stories aloud, with each teen reading a paragraph or two. (Allow teens to pass if they don't want to read.) It takes 10-15 minutes to read a story straight through. However, it is often more effective to let workshop participants make comments and discuss the story as you go along. The workshop leader may even want to annotate her copy of the story beforehand with key questions.

If teens read the story ahead of time or silently, it's good to break the ice with a few questions that get everyone on the same page: Who is the main character? How old is she? What happened to her? How did she respond? Another good starting question is: "What stood out for you in the story?" Go around the room and let each person briefly mention one thing.

Then move on to open-ended questions, which encourage participants to think more deeply about what the writers were feeling, the choices they faced, and the actions they took. There are no right or wrong answers to the open-ended questions.

Open-ended questions encourage participants to think about how the themes, emotions, and choices in the stories relate to their own lives. Here are some examples of open-ended questions that we have found to be effective. You can use variations of these questions with almost any story in this book.

—What main problem or challenge did the writer face?
—What choices did the teen have in trying to deal with the problem?
—Which way of dealing with the problem was most effective for the teen? Why?
—What strengths, skills, or resources did the teen use to address the challenge?
—If you were in the writer's shoes, what would you have done?
—What could adults have done better to help this young person?
—What have you learned by reading this story that you didn't know before?
—What, if anything, will you do differently after reading this story?
—What surprised you in this story?
—Do you have a different view of this issue, or see a different way of dealing with it, after reading this story? Why or why not?

CREDITS

The stories in this book originally appeared in the following Youth Communication publications: "Tales of a 17-Year-Old Smoker" by Edwin Mercado, *New Youth Connections*, December 2000; "Stop the Smoke!" by Evelyn Gofman, *New Youth Connections*, September/October 2002; "How I Quit Fast Food" by Carmen Rios, *New Youth Connections*, May/June 2006; "Clean and Kind of Sober" by Antwaun Garcia, *Represent*, May/June 2005; "What Drugs Do to You," *Represent*, November/December 2007; "Starving for Acceptance" by Anonymous, *New Youth Connections*, December, 2004; "Shapin' Up!" by Antwaun Garcia, *Represent*, September, October 2003; "Addled on Adderall," by Anonymous, YCteen, September/October 2013; "Dear Food Diary" by Various Writers, *New Youth Connections*, September/October, 2009; "Gluttony Getaway" by Elsa Ho, *New Youth Connections*, September/October, 2009; "I Desperately Needed Cooking 101" by Hattie Rice, *Represent*, January/February 2005; "What's Wrong With Fast Food?" by Carmen Rios, New Youth Connections, May/June, 2006; "Why is Bad Food So Good?" by Chantal Hylton, *New Youth Connections*, September/October, 2009; "Why Should Teens Care About Nutrition?" by Stephanie Hinkson, *Represent*, January/February 2005; "My Hood is Bad for My Health" by Anonymous, *Represent*, January/February 2005; "Male on the Scale" by Anonymous, *New Youth Connections*, May/June, 2000; "Scaling Back" by Erica Harrigan, *Represent*, January/February 2005; "The Would-Be Vegetarian" by Suzy Berkowitz, *New Youth Connections*, September/October, 2009; "Carnivore No More," by Kamaal Dashiem Crumpton, *Represent*, Winter 2011; "A Tale of Two Food Chains," *New Youth Connections*, September/October, 2009; "More Tips on Healthy Eating," *New Youth Connections*, September/October, 2009; "I Won't Let Asthma Control My Life" by Viveca Shearin, *New Youth Connections*, March 2008; "How to Breathe Easier" by Natalie Olivero, *New Youth Connections*, September/October, 2006; "Arthritis at 13" by Cantel Morel, *New Youth Communications*, February/March 2011; "My Life with OCD" by Anonymous, *YCteen*, May/June 2016; "Worst. Year. Ever. My Struggle with Scoliosis" by Hande Erkan, *YCteen*, May/June 2017; "Handball Takes Away My Troubles" by Cynthia Orbes, *Represent*, November/December 2003; "How Exercise Relieves Stress" by Nakese Bullock, *Represent*, November/December 2003; "Yoga Relaxes Me" by Niya Wilson, *New Youth Connections*, April 2000; "Poetry Keeps Me Calm" by Ashunte Hunt, *Represent*, September/October 2007; "Do for You" by Shante Brown, *New Youth Connections*, March 2000; "Nature is My Salvation" by Emily Orchier, *New Youth Connections*, April 2000;

About Youth Communication

Youth Communication, founded in 1980, is a nonprofit professional development organization serving middle school and high school educators. It provides compelling true stories by teens, professional development, social and emotional learning curricula, and anthologies. The teen-written stories in this book were developed in Youth Communication's intensive, year-round writing workshops. The stories make it easy for educators to bring compelling youth voices directly into their classrooms, including the voices of students who are least likely to feel represented in school. The vast majority of Youth Communication writers are youth of color; many have experienced other challenges related to foster care, homelessness, immigration status, gender, and sexuality. In their stories, the teens show how they use one or more of the CASEL social and emotional learning competencies (self-awareness, self-management, social awareness, relationships, and responsible decision-making) to manage challenges and achieve their goals. As such, they are instructive and inspiring to teens and helpful tools for educators. Youth Communication's fully scripted grade 6 to 12 advisory curricula help educators connect with the youth they serve and transform classrooms and schools into dynamic, engaging learning environments. For more information about our resources and professional development offerings, go to youthcomm.org.

About the Editors

Al Desetta has been an editor of Youth Communication's two teen magazines, Foster Care Youth United (now known as Represent) and New Youth Connections. He was also an instructor in Youth Communication's juvenile prison writing program. In 1991, he became the organization's first director of teacher development, working with high school teachers to help them produce better writers and student publications.

Prior to working at Youth Communication, Desetta directed environmental education projects in New York City public high schools and worked as a reporter.

He has a master's degree in English literature from City College of the City University of New York and a bachelor's degree from the State University of New York at Binghamton, and he was a Revson Fellow at Columbia University for the 1990–91 academic year.

He is the editor of many books, including several other Youth Communication anthologies: *The Heart Knows Something Different: Teenage Voices from the Foster Care System*, *The Struggle to Be Strong*, and *The Courage to Be Yourself*. He is currently a freelance editor.

Keith Hefner co-founded Youth Communication in 1980 and has directed it ever since. He is the recipient of the Luther P. Jackson Education Award from the New York Association of Black Journalists and a MacArthur Fellowship. He was also a Revson Fellow at Columbia University.

Laura Longhine is the editorial director at Youth Communication. She edited Represent, Youth Communication's magazine by and for youth in foster care, for three years, and has written for a variety of publications. She has a BA in English from Tufts University and an MS in Journalism from Columbia University.